Table of Contents

Chapter 1:

1998 - 2001

Think Different Than the World

JUST AS IT IS WRITTEN, THINGS WHICH EYE HAS NOT SEEN AND EAR HAS NOT HEARD, AND WHICH HAVE NOT ENTERED THE HEART OF MAN, ALL THAT GOD HAS PREPARED FOR THOSE WHO LOVE HIM. 1 CORINTHIANS 2:9 NASB

This story is about my life, but it's God's story. It's the true story of how God called me back to Himself. Before I found God, I was an abusive, drug-addicted sexual predator determined to destroy my life. I was addicted to the worst kinds of pornography, prostitution, and drugs. No one wanted to be near me or get to know who I was. This is how God changed me from the inside out and brought me back to life.

Life is full of blessings if you know where to look for them. My pastor calls them "God Winks." In all the years I have lived on this earth, there have been no real coincidences, but there have been many instances of God intervening in things I thought were out of His control.

Time and experience play a huge part in shaping our beliefs. God has shown me great grace throughout my life, and I want to share my story of how He took me out of the pit of hell and led me back to His kingdom.

Might As Well Face it!

This is a story about overcoming my sins. It wasn't my own doing, but the power of Jesus Christ was interwoven into my life throughout the years. In my story, you will see the pain and suffering I endured while running out of the pit of hell and just how deadly sin can be.

This is a story of how God brought me out of my addiction to pornography, drugs, alcohol, and prostitution. If you read it to the end, I assure you that you will see a different person than the one you initially read about. God makes all things new. Here is the rest of God's story about my life and how I returned to Jesus' protection.

After high school, I thought I had freedom. I thought I would be able to make my own decisions, get out of my parent's basement, out of their shadow of protection, and live on my own without enduring further abuse from my relatives. Little did I know that the world was just as broken outside as inside my home; Only I didn't know who the players were or who I could trust.

On the surface, I projected an intimidating persona about myself. I was successful in scaring acquaintances, who, in reality, were much sicker than I was, into thinking I was crazy and beyond repair. I learned this defense as a child to protect me most of my life. If people thought I was crazy, then they would leave me alone. My actions were driven by a need to protect myself, much like King David pretended to be insane to safeguard himself from his enemies.

I was always afraid of the world because of the abuse I endured in the home from people who weren't my parents. I saw that the world wasn't much different outside my family home, so I retreated into the places and spaces I could control and keep myself as safe as I knew how to be. I became aggressive with pornography and sex as my weapons of choice, but I never let my guard down, and I wasn't about to bring myself to normalcy.

In my mind, being kind was a sign of weakness, and I learned I couldn't be vulnerable toward anyone. Anyone kind toward me was questionable, and I felt they had a deeper motive to hurt me and turn on me when I wasn't looking. So, I tried to keep my distance from those people. For me, a church was just a place to pick up women as vulnerable as I was.

I viewed the world as a mere toy, something I could manipulate and control to suit my desires without regard for a higher power. After all, how could a benevolent God allow me to endure such prolonged suffering? I was determined to seek retribution upon the world for how it had treated me.

Despite struggling to focus, I was determined to pursue a career similar to my successful brother's. He had excelled as a computer programmer with a business degree, and following in his footsteps might have brought me the same success. At the time, making my parents proud was important to me, so I became a computer programmer with a business degree.

As a young student, I dreamed of becoming a successful musician. Sadly, those dreams were shattered when I witnessed my older brother struggling in college. I couldn't help but doubt my abilities - if he couldn't make it, how could I? Despite my brother's natural musical talent, my parents often reminded me of his academic struggles, urging me to be more realistic about my future. They warned me that the music industry was highly competitive and that only exceptional talents could succeed. As a result, I began to question whether I had what it takes to make it in such a cutthroat business.

After my senior year in high school, my music teacher received an invitation for her students to perform at a world-famous music hall in New York City. I was lucky enough to be selected as one of the performers. I and seven other classmates were invited to go and sing in New York City. We had to practice day and night after school for six months straight. Finally, we were ready to fly to the Big Apple and perform for thousands of people. All of this was to have a life-changing experience in the music industry.

I remember seeing an elderly lady outside the back door of the theatre, dressed in clothes made of garbage bags, begging for help. Being from a smaller city, I had never seen homelessness on that scale before. We were warned not to look at anyone directly and to avoid speaking to strangers as it would surely lead to being kidnapped or killed. It was all an experience that made me feel mature beyond my years. However, once I stepped onto the stage to perform, I was fully immersed in the moment and didn't think about anything else.

Watching the three thousand men and women cheer for me while the choir sang classical music was an incredibly moving experience. It made me feel like music was my calling. It was like God was calling me to break out of the shadow I had fallen under in chasing my parents' dream for my life. I was called to move to New York City and start a music career.

However, it was also the last time I could recall feeling God's presence.

At the concert, I was also introduced to a highly inappropriate game. The singers would dare each other to sing loud to the wrong word and see if anyone could hear it and not get caught. It just so happened that I was the loudest, and the last note of a song drew silence. My words echoed throughout the theatre hall, only to be overlooked by the crowd's applause.

After that experience, I lived at home with my parents while I attended a community college in my hometown. It wasn't much of a college at the time, but it was gaining a reputation for hiring local talents straight into the workforce of insurance companies and banks in our city. My brother had already attended there after failing out of two other schools and drinking and partying his way out the college doors.

He went into the military for about four years of active duty and then went into the Guard. There, he traveled the world and met many women. All the while, he was struggling with a girlfriend at home who was very twisted in her mind and trying to cause him trouble. This was while I was still in high school. But after he got out of the military, he found himself returning to school and getting hired on by one of the biggest companies in the area, so it became a massive goal for my parents to push the same successes onto me.

After graduating from high school, I began to view life from a different perspective. I missed my friends and the strong bonds we had created. There were several friends I wanted to keep in touch with, but for various reasons, it wasn't easy. I even dreamed about returning to high school for another year because I had failed some courses and wanted to help my favorite teacher teach music.

I visited some of my classmates several times, but eventually, I had to move on from that phase of my life after two years. My former choir director decided to retire from the school system in our city and transition to a new career as a student counselor. I admired her decision and believed she could make an even greater impact on students by helping them in ways that music could not always achieve.

In the fall of that year, I enrolled in my first computer class in college and immediately developed a passion for learning about technology. Growing up, I had played all of the original home entertainment consoles and knew how much fun they were, which ultimately drew me towards the computer industry. Although I was already well-versed in computers during high school, I secured my first real job in the technology field with the help of a college professor. I found a position at a local big box store, which began my career in the technology industry.

In my young and impressionable mind, I thought I had landed the most incredible job in the world. And indeed, it was an exciting time for me. I learned a great deal about technology and interacting with people. Being naive, I listened carefully to my trainers and absorbed everything like a sponge. I started to let my guard down and let others into my life.

I learned about hardware, software, and printers and even acquired the skills to sell things to people who didn't need them. All of this was thanks to some of the best retail sales teams in the country at the time. However, little did I know that this career would lead me down a path that would challenge my morality even further than it was broken before.

The job itself wasn't the problem, but it put me in some of the most unpleasant living situations I had ever experienced. During my time there, I was exposed to illegal activities such as piracy, immoral behavior, people scamming each other, and cut-throat tactics like those used during Black Friday sales. I learned about things on the Internet that shouldn't even exist in the natural world, and I was caught in the world of extreme pornography. If it was on the Internet somewhere, I wanted to find it.

As a salesperson, I was trained to use various techniques to convince customers to purchase equipment they didn't need or couldn't afford. Initially, it seemed like a fun challenge, but soon, I realized I would have to compromise my moral values to excel at this job. The pressure to sell at any cost took me to a dark place where I had to abandon my morals. Unfortunately, such unethical practices were becoming increasingly common in those days. It was like I was living a double life. I sold to people daily, duping them out of money, and then went home at night to look at the worst things I could find online. I was digging a huge, limitless hole of despair and destruction.

I had the privilege of having many great teachers in retail, one of whom was my manager in the computer sales department at the time. He took me under his wing and showed me how the sales team could function like a family and how success could be achieved when everyone worked together. Although it was a great learning experience, a huge part of me didn't want to be part of that particular 'family.'

They drank and partied all the time and played video games until the next morning. They showed me how to get to the worst parts of the Internet behind closed doors. They were just like my abusive family, except without the additional sexual abuse. I often wondered if I would see an old picture of myself as a child in one of the pictures.

Fortunately, the upper management teams realized the chaos family-style leadership brought was counterproductive and decided to separate us. This diluted the closeness we had previously shared, and we returned to the old tactics of cutthroat sales, which they called the 'care method' of sales.

I decided to gain more experience in the company by becoming a team lead and moving to the car audio department. I had no prior knowledge about this area except for the daily bass blasts from the subwoofer section of the car audio area and the teenagers who wanted to have the loudest music possible, making them the coolest kids in town and the target of the next street gang's theft list. Their experiences of wanting the loudest car in town changed when someone stole their equipment, and they had to return to replace it within a week.

After working in the car audio department, the management team thought that it would be a good idea for me to try my talents in the car audio installation bay for approximately three months. The experience there was quite shocking. The work culture was such that if you were unwell, you could not call in sick because you were expected to vomit outside and continue working once you were finished.

During that time, I also started smoking and drinking, but I didn't enjoy it very much. Working in that position made me feel extremely angry and bitter towards the world, as did the other installers. I bought my tools and lost most of them over time. I had to buy my own mechanics box and spend thousands of dollars I didn’t have to spend. It was like I was on an island of misfit toys. So I decided to go back onto the sales floor.

As I moved up in the store's roles, I purchased a new truck to impress my colleagues after my last two cars had died. It was all white, with steel rims, a premium sound system, and a black bed topper. But I was in an accident before I installed the topper and a security system.

I was coming home from work when a traffic jam occurred. Several cars were involved in an accident ahead of me, and behind me were speeding people trying to get home from a busy work day. As I slowed down, a car came up behind me and slammed into my rear bumper, shattering my tailgate and pushing the bed of my truck into the back of the cab ever so slightly.

The car and driver running into me backed up and tried to escape the traffic quickly. He was quickly caught by people trying to flag him down, and they received a partial license plate number and gave it to me as I was taken away by ambulance due to a headache from the tensing up of my body during the impact.

The police put a broadcast to find the vehicle that hit my truck and couldn't find him after he fled the scene. The next day, however, I drove my parent's van to work and saw a vehicle being ditched on the side of the road heading into my store. The man was ditching the car that hit me with his father in front of a miniature golf course.

It turned out he was running from the accident because he had 300 pounds of cocaine in the back of his trunk and didn't want to get caught. I pulled off to the other side of the road and watched as the police came and quickly surrounded the man's vehicle, and the place became a crime scene.

A few months later, after getting my truck back from being repaired, I left it parked in the street only for the night, and someone stole my new tailgate. A few days later, that same tailgate was found on the back of a dark blue truck that didn't quite fit its model, and my girlfriend and parents followed the truck to a soccer field and called the police. The young man quickly told me that he had bought it from some random guy and hadn't known it had been stolen. The police then asked for their names, or he was going to jail, and I was given back my tailgate.

The truck stood as a monument to what God does to those who mess with His children. Only I didn't want to believe in God at the time. Even though I had a girlfriend, I went to church to impress girls. My experiences with women up to that point were that you needed as many as possible. My experience in the big-box store echoed that same value system.

My final position in that store was in the appliance area. I liked working there. It was the most effortless roll in the store. Most people knew what they wanted and came in, and I helped them put in the order for it and carried it to their vehicles. It was a place of being laid back and having fun. I didn't feel as pressured to sell to others here, but something was missing.

One day, I attended an appliance conference at a hotel with my coworkers. There, we had a lot of drinks, and one of the coworkers brought up the idea that we should go to a strip club. I was trapped with them for the ride and agreed. We left and went to the club, to the tune of $200.00 out of my pocket and a girl's phone number, only to discover it was fake. I returned the next day to realize she had taken my money and run away, leaving me chasing my tail. After that experience, I returned to the computer sales team.

Upon returning to the computer sales floor with a new team, I realized that the atmosphere didn’t have the family and team spirit I had experienced the times before. The new manager solely focused on merchandise sales and limited our ability to help each other. The Internet had taken over how we sold machines, and most customers only wanted a free computer when they signed up for a three-year contract with dial-up Internet services. I noticed that the industry was changing rapidly during my six months away.

Might As Well Face it!

I didn't know how the team turned out, but I wondered where my next step would be if I were to leave the big box store. I left college to work full-time for a company I didn't think had my best interests at heart, and I wanted to do something great with my life! Little did I know that I was up for a wild ride that would lead me back to the cross of Jesus Christ. But I had to go through a lot of pain first. One morning, I prayed that God would use me to change the world and help me become as popular as a rock star.

After the Y2K scare had passed, I found myself in a position where I needed to reassess my skills and determine what direction to take next. Programmers were being laid off because their expertise was no longer in high demand. Their primary value was fixing the clock glitch that occurred in the year 2000. This was due to a lazy programming habit where computers used only double-digits for the year field inside dates. Although the glitch only affected one operating system, businesses used it more frequently, so it required a prompt fix. I vividly remember this period because some religious fanatics were predicting that it was the end of the world and that Jesus was returning. Fortunately, this did not happen.

I had become cold and hard-hearted towards God due to my past experiences and a lack of faith. Everything from being subjected to child abuse to viewing different types of pornography has left me feeling numb. Moreover, the doomsday rumors turned out to be false, which left a bad taste in my mouth for the church. I was so deep in the darkness of sin that it seemed almost no light was left. I was living with my girlfriend in my parent's basement and engaging in online relationships with women in chat rooms. This was something I had learned to do from my previous job at the big box store.

One night, I applied for a new job with a company I had never heard of before. Later, I received a call from a woman who claimed to be from a California-based company with the motto “Don’t think like the rest of the world." At first, I was confused and wondered why they would call me. Then, I realized I had applied to a recruiting company that worked with the larger corporation.

During the interview, I expressed my misunderstanding, thinking the call was a joke and that the company was going out of business. However, they assured me they were not going out of business and that I was a good fit for the position. Even though their approach was unconventional, just like any of their marketing ploys, after learning all the details about the job, I felt like I had won the lottery.

I was sent to California to work with the CEO and the product development teams to learn how to sell their products. However, I had no idea this experience would become the darkest point of my life. I didn’t want anything to do with God or the church; I had become indifferent towards people. Nevertheless, God answered my prayer about changing the world and becoming as popular as a rock star.

Might As Well Face it!

Chapter 2:

2001 - 2002

Finding Solutions

[3] I WAS WITH YOU IN WEAKNESS AND IN FEAR AND IN MUCH TREMBLING, [4] AND MY MESSAGE AND MY PREACHING WERE NOT IN PERSUASIVE WORDS OF WISDOM, BUT IN DEMONSTRATION OF THE SPIRIT AND OF POWER, [5]SO THAT YOUR FAITH WOULD NOT REST ON THE WISDOM OF MEN, BUT ON THE POWER OF GOD. 1 CORINTHIANS 2:3-5

For the first time, I traveled alone, without any loved ones accompanying me. I had a short layover in Dallas, Texas, where I made small talk with total strangers. Airport security was relatively easy to pass through, and people were busy with their lives. I was filled with adrenaline and excitement as I was about to meet with a company that would later revolutionize the computing technology industry for years.

I finally landed at the airport in San Diego and found my chauffeur, who drove me to the campus. I had been in this vast new city for a week alone and had no idea what was in store for me in this new role.

The driver took me on a two-hour journey through the city out into the country, and back to a Beverly Hills-looking area. Finally, we arrived at a glass building with a white company logo in the center. I found myself in the heart of Silicon Valley. All the major tech companies were lined up along the side of the road. I recognized several names that jumped out from the pages of the Internet. It was a computer nerd's dream town. The only issue I had was that the town looked abandoned.

After the year 2000, many programmers and businesses encountered challenges because there was no longer a need to fix the Y2K bug. The computing industry was advancing toward new frontiers, and "Dial-up" Internet Service Providers were becoming less popular. Cable television companies were entering the Internet market along with DSL services from phone companies. In contrast, Internet speeds were faster than dial-up services but also expensive. Cell phones were used to make phone calls, but personal digital assistant technology was rising.

I arrived at the companies' ground level, which sparked the computer boom from 1984 to 2001. The driver asked me to get out of the car and go to the front door to meet the rest of the team. The teams were gathered around a central location in a grassy field beyond the gigantic glass building. Security was tight and technology-forward even for a company of its size.

Guards watched our every move, and security cameras were strategically placed to monitor everyone nearby. Metal detectors, facial recognition, and fingerprint scanners ensured people were who they said they were. Before entering, each employee received a picture badge with a radio transmitter, and a system scan showed where a person was at all times. The doors were electronically coded and required the correct key and bio-scan access for entry. The efficiency with which everything worked was truly impressive.

A security guard interrupted, looking around, "Right this way, sir! Please show the security desk your photo ID, and they will give you your badge." "Before you go in, we need you to sign some waivers and nondisclosure agreements to keep everything confidential," announced one of the senior directors. "So, if you could form a line, we will have you fill out the papers and then come into the conference room." We quickly lined up and signed our lives away for what lay behind the door.

We all entered a darkened room, walking in single file to a round of cheering, clapping, and loud music that seemed more like a party than the first day of work. It was unlike anything I had ever experienced. We were taken to the front of the room and displayed for the rest of the people to see. I found myself in the center of the crowd on the big stage, wondering what would happen. Then, the CEO came on stage to introduce what we were there to do.

After all the cheering, clapping, and music had calmed down, the CEO explained why we had all gathered there and were being applauded so gratefully. The meeting managers announced that we were the second phase of a group that would forever change the world of computing. The first phase saw exponential growth just by the presence of one person in the stores they managed. The company was banking on the next phase to be even better.

We had been chosen to be the face of the company in the real world. Our team was comprised of market researchers, sales experts, and tech specialists, all dedicated to staying ahead in the company's fast-paced markets. The company had ambitious tech ideas, and they wanted us to undergo direct training from top developers to show customers that we were here to make a lasting impact. We aimed to uncover the world's cravings and requirements for cutting-edge technology and then communicate our discoveries to the corporate headquarters.

The company aimed to demonstrate its commitment to thinking outside the box while providing the luxury car experience to its customer base and helping those who didn't know about the technology to switch to our platform. The company even built a campaign around our being present in the stores within the stores. We had access to inside information on various products and services and collected market data intimately. We connected with the people purchasing or not purchasing the products to get their input on why they made their decisions. This data enabled the company to offer valuable insights into what must be done differently to outperform its competition and revitalize its business.

During the last few days of training, a motivational speaker taught us techniques for selling products more efficiently. He showed us how to create images in people's minds, focus on our customers' needs, and maximize their purchases. We were able to give people a vision of how to use the products and services to improve their lives. It was an excellent training session, and I was amazed at the results it brought to our sales. This was far different from my sales experience at my previous job.

After our training sessions ended for the day, the nightlife became quite a wild party. The company ensured we had everything we needed for a great party: an unlimited supply of alcohol, a wide variety of food, and people waiting on us, hand and foot. It was like paradise; I felt on top of the world. We were paired with roommates to stay at the nearby hotels with other team members.

My roommate and I became good friends during the training session. I looked up to him for guidance. I became his wingman during the parties and watched him get the girls. He had the body of a Chip and Dale's dancer. He was from Kansas City but had ties to my hometown in Des Moines. To me, his moves to pick up women were inspiring.

He was a fascinating person with many intriguing qualities. He was very health-conscious and attractive, which constantly caught women's attention. Everywhere we went, a girl would ask for his number, or someone at the bar would try to get his attention. As a 21-year-old man on my own for the first time in another state, the experience was eye-opening. All the adult content I had consumed before I came to work there came to life in my mind. I needed to know his secret!

After the training and the party ended, my roommate and I went to a bar. I got even more drunk and somehow made it back to the hotel, leaving my roommate behind at the bar. Later, he brought a girl from the bar back to our room. I was asleep when they arrived, but their entrance woke me up. At the time, I was curious to see what would happen between my friend and the girl, as I admired his dating skills. I pretended to remain asleep, hoping to witness something exciting between them.

However, things went differently than I had hoped. The girl decided it wasn't right to interact with me in the room, so they called it a night. Sometimes, I think God has a sense of humor in the way he protects us from going down the wrong path. This was one of those times for me. Then again, Satan could have been enticing me to sin further as well.

My roommate asked me if I had heard or seen anything the following day. Quietly, I replied, "Yes, I heard everything, but I wasn't going to say anything. I'm sorry for blocking your action." To my surprise, he responded, "You know you have a girlfriend at home who's missing you, right? I wish I had someone I could be with all the time instead of these women who only want to be with my body for the experience and looks. All they ever want is a piece of meat, and then they throw out the bones once they are done." In my heart, I knew that was exactly what I was doing when I was looking at pornography or looking at women as objects. A part of me said, stop the behavior before it ruins your life.

My friend's words left a huge hole in the pit of my stomach. How could all of those pornographic movies be so wrong about sex and love? All of my thoughts of being a player were shot out the window at that moment. This was the man I had joked around with the night before about how many women he could sleep with. I couldn't believe someone living such a life would say, "I want your life. I'm tired of partying and drinking without having someone to be with." It didn't align with what I believed life was about. I didn't know what to think after that experience.

Was I wrong to treat women the way they were treating me? As objects? Was there more to a relationship than just sex and mind games? I couldn't get those thoughts out of my head and questioned my morals at that moment, but I quickly went back to what I knew and went to sleep.

The past four years of consuming Internet pornography had a detrimental impact on my well-being, transforming me into a person I despised. During my time working at the big box store, I encountered numerous individuals who indulged in various forms of pornography on the internet. They amassed thousands of hours of explicit content, and I found myself immersed in that culture. Then I conversed with the one man who appeared deeply entrenched in this lifestyle, only to discover that he loathed his existence.

Listening to him speak, I couldn't help but reflect on how I had been living my life. I had witnessed so many people modeling their lives after figures like Hugh Hefner and pornographic movie stars. While it might have appeared glamorous on the surface, the reality was that it destroyed lives, belittled men and women, and hurt the world around them. Despite this, I didn't want to face the truth about that lifestyle. But there it was, staring me in the face. I had to either confront it or ignore its presence and let it consume me further.

I took those thoughts home with me after leaving California. I was so eager to succeed that as soon as I returned from my training, I wasted no time diving into work. I completely ignored the lesson I had just learned about living for others' well-being. When I landed back in town, I went to the store and asked the sales team how my company's products were selling. All the while still objectifying women and being conflicted with my friend's words.

The store was a retail disaster. A ladder blocked the view of the hardware section. The product line was displayed incorrectly, and the employees could have done better to inform customers about the selections offered. When I asked for their recommendations on a computer, no one mentioned our company until I asked for the product's name. Even then, it was an uphill battle.

After browsing the store, I introduced myself to the store manager and explained why I was there. The store manager warmly greeted me, showed me around, introduced me to the team, and helped me get my bearings. After that, I was off to a great start.

I worked with the staff to clean up the area. We got marketing materials that shined and attracted the buyers to the area of the store where our products were. We got the ladder out of the center aisle and worked with the staff to get more informed on the hardware and software solutions my company was offering. We worked the store to the top sales team in the region.

After consistently ranking among the company's top salespeople for about seven months, our leadership changed. We were summoned to a meeting in Chicago and informed about restructuring our leadership. The company determined that a more sophisticated and professional approach was necessary, and we were given new team managers.

I vividly remember the impact our new team manager had when he entered the store. He was a real New Yorker from the Bronx with a loud and energetic personality that could rub anyone wrong, including the store management team I led. I faced a challenging task, but he immediately made his presence known with a spirited entrance. He came to see the top salesperson on his team, a position I had achieved through hard work, and I was eager to learn how to improve further. He was determined to implement changes that would make our team the best in the company.

I followed his plans, mostly because I needed to learn about selling to businesses. I listened to his advice and absorbed his knowledge as much as possible. We had several meetings and worked to prepare the team for larger commissions and sales with bigger companies. Everything was going to be bigger and better than before.

I was fully committed to the journey. I aimed to conduct thorough research and bring a high level of professionalism to my work. However, when my sales declined, I realized the importance of understanding how to work with and sell to businesses. This led me to return to school and complete my degree in Business Administration. That was my first mistake.

With my new manager at the helm, he demanded more of my time and wondered about my loyalty. He expressed pride in my decision to return to school but emphasized the need to focus on the bigger picture. As the inventory manager, I assumed a more prominent role in my team as we prepared for the holiday season.

Our next business practice training was once again in Chicago. This time, we were tasked with developing a team-building exercise to unite the team. Similar to my experience at the previous big-box store, I had a new nickname: A.D.D. Boy. I even had a bright red shirt with black letters on the back to prove it. I was assigned a new role as the inventory manager for the entire region. I was responsible for tracking inventory and redistributing products to boost sales for stores with lower inventory levels.

I was allowed to secure one of the most important sales our company had ever seen in the area. The task was to set up an employee purchase program with a large firm that exclusively used our systems. I needed prior experience in this area to feel prepared to take on such a significant role, and unfortunately, I failed. Despite putting in a lot of effort to make the sale as smooth as possible, my lack of experience led to difficulties handling such a large account.

I researched the deal and even arranged with the store's general manager to offer a small discount to secure a larger sale with the client. The store's general manager was new, having recently relocated from another state. He had a sophisticated taste and was accustomed to having the best of everything in his life. I believed the store manager was there to help me finalize this deal.

Might As Well Face it!

The new store manager set me up for failure. He thought the Solutions Consultants were a joke and a waste of time and money. He wanted to see the whole program fail from the start. I listened to his advice, thinking it came from a credible source with influence in the business world. In reality, he had his ideas about success.

I suggested contacting a large publishing company to discuss implementing an employee purchase program. The program would offer discounts to employees, increasing sales at our store. I planned to present the company with an employee discount program, become their dedicated local vendor for all purchases, and offer better deals than they were currently getting online. Despite my enthusiasm for the idea, the manager only offered a 5% discount on computer hardware and no discount on major software.

I tried to reason with the general manager that this needed to be improved. I tried to explain to him that we would look like fools going in with this low amount, but that was all they would give me. There was an 11 million dollar sale on the line. Plus, all the sales the employee purchase program would have provided to the store foot traffic. The General Manager didn't want to see it for what it was. The store didn't budge, and I lost the sale on the store's end.

It made me look horrible as a business salesperson, and I ultimately lost my job. I was told that what I wore to the meeting broke the deal and that I looked like a fool, rather than the fact that they didn't provide me with any leverage to gain a customer of such a high caliber.

Unfortunately, I didn't see the termination coming shortly after that. All I knew was that I was exhausted from working long hours and feeling humiliated by a sale that didn't go as planned. My manager came to my store to take me out to eat wherever I wanted. He said to think big, and he would foot the bill.

In reality, he had some bad news for me. He told me in no uncertain terms that I had to quit immediately or face being fired in three months, blaming me for the company's loss. I was devastated and felt like a failure. The steak I ate made me sick with anxiety, and I had to take a week off work to recover. I had to go home and tell my family I lost my job but was offered a local position in the retail store. I was back to square one.

Despite my shock, I remained in the store and shadowed my former roommate, whom I had met in California. I accepted the deal my manager gave me, even though I could have claimed unemployment benefits. I was proud and wanted to keep my dignity more than the money, which was more important than relying on unemployment benefits.

I became aware of my manager's betrayal when I found out he had arranged a meeting with the company that ended my career. The meeting involved creating the employee purchase program and keeping the commissions for himself.

He knew I couldn't handle the pressure and planned to return my former roommate to take over my position. This would allow my former roommate to dominate the sales from the corner area I had worked hard to develop from scratch. I felt frustrated and resentful about how they treated me, and I felt like I was worse than a criminal.

I was given a chance to follow my former roommate as an apprentice and learn about the business side of sales for the company, with the possibility of eventually returning to work for them later on after I had gained more experience.

Chapter 3:

2003 - 2004

Leaving the Company

[15]DO NOT LOVE THE THINGS OF THE WORLD OR THE THINGS IN THE WORLD. IF ANYONE LOVES THE WORLD, THE LOVE OF THE FATHER IS NOT IN HIM. [16]FOR ALL THAT IS IN THE WORLD, THE LUST OF THE FLESH AND THE LUST OF THE EYES AND THE BOASTFUL PRIDE OF LIFE, IS NOT FROM THE FATHER, BUT IS FROM THE WORLD. 1 JOHN 2:15-16 NASB

After being fired, I struggled to accept the loss. I wanted to stay but knew I couldn't rectify the missed deal. The $11 million sale went to the original salesperson, and my manager shared the commission for rescuing it. I was offered a job as an associate to my training partner, who supported my return if an opportunity arose.

My friend moved into the store to build upon the foundation I had set, aiming to achieve even greater success. The manager agreed that I would continue to be involved in team meetings and contribute to helping my former roommate deliver outstanding sales results, further propelling the store's growth. This was an excellent chance to expand my business sales knowledge and learn from the team's top-performing salesperson. The end goal was that my former roommate would become the next team manager and that I would be brought back as the solutions consultant of the store again.

Might As Well Face it!

I came across an advertisement for a prescription drug designed for Adult Attention Deficit Disorder (ADD). My former boss used to call me "ADD boy," and I had the T-shirt to prove it. The ad caught my interest. I wondered if I had this issue and if medication could help me get my old job back. If I could work better and impress my former boss, I would have a chance to regain my old job.

I made a lot of mistakes during that time in my life. A few weeks before I left the company, I followed my father's advice and sold my truck to buy a newer, fancier Chevy Blazer with all the bells and whistles. It would impress our new clients and help me make a good impression. Unfortunately, the deal fell through, leaving me with a huge debt. On top of that, I had to pay over $6000 in taxes to the IRS for my final commission checks that year.

I also decided to have Lasik surgery to improve my eyesight because I was nearly blind in both eyes. I was insecure about my appearance and thought glasses did little to enhance it. That year, my girlfriend and I also got married in a big wedding with around 300 guests, trying to impress everyone. I was so caught up in my vanity that I didn't think about the thousands of dollars left in my checking account.

I went to my family doctor to ask for a test to diagnose ADD. The doctor mentioned that it would have been better if I had been diagnosed earlier in life, as it would have helped me academically and in general. The doctor told me that ADD is a newly diagnosed condition that affects many individuals. He recommended that I start a medication treatment for Adult

ADD symptoms, which could improve my alertness, academic performance, and job performance.

I expressed my concerns to the doctor about taking medication for the rest of my life and being labeled as "broken." Despite my reluctance, the doctor recommended that I try the treatment anyway. He told me that it would take four weeks to get used to the effects of the medication and advised me not to consume alcohol or over-the-counter cough syrup containing alcohol. I didn't have any alcohol in my house because my girlfriend's parents were alcoholics, and I didn't want to take any risks.

Taking the medications, I could see improvements in my concentration, and my attention to detail improved. In several meetings, I contributed ideas to improve the team's performance and attract more professional clients. I also aimed to revamp the store's appearance within the larger chain store and brought several new ideas to the store's merchandising. However, the local general store manager had a way of undercutting his team, which I experienced firsthand. He was the reason I ended up losing the $11 million sale, but I quickly forgave him for making things harder in my life.

During one of the meetings with my old company, I was encouraged to give some ideas on improving our technology. I listened as we thought about new types of hardware and software that still needed to be given as a solution. I suggested we build our own version of a smartphone, which would be our design, and it could be a touch screen with a single button in case the screen fails. That way, the programmers could create their own buttons and functionality without being constrained to one type of hardware design.

I was told they would recommend it to the company's owners and let me know what they came back with. The next week, I was in the meeting and told that they were in the process of making such a device and that I needed to leave the meeting. I quickly asked if it would be a touch screen like I had suggested, as the CEO was on the call. Then, the door slammed in my face.

Returning to the sales floor, I saw the writing on the wall. I knew I wasn't going back to my old job. I had burned a lot of bridges, and the new medications were working almost too well. My concentration was improving, and I was depressed. I wanted to improve my appearance by undergoing Lasik surgery before our wedding day, so I scheduled a consultation with my eye doctor. I paid cash with the rest of the money left from the remainder of the last commission check.

Just before the surgery, I had very poor vision in both of my eyes with a prescription of -9 and -8. I had to wear thick glasses; I could only see blurry outlines without them. However, after the surgery, I achieved 20/20 vision and could immediately see the clock on the wall. My eyes were sore for a day but returned to normal afterward. With eye drops and other treatments, I had to take care of them for a while, but it was worth it. I could see my face with just two eyes instead of four for the first time.

As my girlfriend and I planned our wedding, we realized that getting married meant buying a house and moving out of my parents' basement. This would be the first time I had ever left the comfort and protection of their home despite having traveled the world. I had never lived outside my parents' house. So we found a home close by, allowing me to remain close to the comforts of the area, not to mention all of our friends and family near us.

I had perceived the area as a place of comfort, but I eventually realized it was an illusion. My family home had been a hiding place for the secrets of my past abuse by my family. Moving out of my comfort zone and into a new place made me realize how broken I was. All the decisions, in reality, overwhelmed me, and I was unsure whether it was depression or if my medications were causing some issues.

Not realizing what the medications did for my memory, I kept using them to improve my concentration, and it also made me more arrogant. Behind closed doors, I was a scared rabbit looking at pornography because I couldn't sleep, and it became my only comfort. And I couldn't keep from concentrating on things as the days passed. I kept going deeper and deeper into a dark hole. The pornography was getting darker. I couldn't break away from it. I was finding myself getting irritable with my friends and family. I even yelled at my girlfriend that, in my mind, I felt like nothing was wrong with what I was doing, but deep down, I knew I was getting worse.

One evening, I lost my temper with my friends after they discovered my pornography usage. Weeks before the wedding, everything fell apart. We had just moved into a new home, and life was starting to settle down. We argued about my emotional distance from everyone, and I realized I couldn't keep my secret any longer. All the abuse, neglect, and trauma from my past came tumbling out in a burst of anger.

That night, I had a terrifying nightmare about the abuse I suffered from my brother, which I had kept hidden from everyone. Being away from home for the first time, I realized I was safe but still causing pain to others. I recognized that I had pushed away those who were there to protect me, and I broke down, crying for what felt like hours. When my girlfriend asked me what was wrong, I told her everything I had done and was still doing up until that point.

In the admission of the hurt, I felt a huge weight lifted off my chest. My family could no longer hurt me. I was out of the house it all happened in, and I was rid of the guilt and shame because it was out in the open. I went back to my family doctor that same week and asked if I could get some counseling and who he would recommend. I explained all that had happened to me over the years, and the medical chart history even proved my behaviors. He could see the writing on the wall but couldn't say anything due to HIPAA rules at that time.

He recommended an older lady counselor and said she was the best for adults who were traumatized from child abuse. I went to the appointment and told her everything. I told her about how I had been looking at the darkest parts of the Internet and that I had been sexual with my nephew several years before. She quickly became angry at me and told me I should have been locked away and the key thrown away. I couldn't argue with her much, but at the same time, her advice didn't help my confidence to get help and counseling. So I did what any good traumatized person would do at that moment: I tucked it back into my pocket, went out the door, and went on about my life like nothing had ever happened.

The medications were working very well for the time and, at the same time, almost too well to accommodate what took place with my friends. They didn't show up to the wedding because my behavior was off the wall terrible. I couldn't believe my behavior and wondered where it came from. I decided to have a party, invite all of them over after we got back from the honeymoon, and bring all the drinks they wanted. We were going to have a party.

I quickly realized why my doctor had advised me not to drink alcohol while taking my medications. It made me behave inappropriately and say things I would never say when sober. It caused me to act out of character, although I didn't realize it then. When my friends pointed it out, I passed out, and everyone left for the night.

My friends and I quickly made amends and got back to normal gatherings. I grew tired of being a salesperson and decided to take a more non-commission sales role in the computer store. I could make more money in customer service than selling to shoppers, and I wanted a break from the unpredictable outcome of my commissions.

While working in customer service, I quickly advanced my career. I worked in the merchandise team before becoming a team leader once again. I regained my confidence and found that the medications were helping me. One day, I overheard a conversation between a business sales representative and someone discussing a new opportunity with another company. It was for a position at a security tech company, and they were specifically looking for someone new to the technology field whom they could train to work on installations. Earlier that year, I had decided to return to school to complete my business administration degree and pursue new opportunities.

I left the retail business and became an installer for security hardware and equipment. I climbed ladders and ran cables. I learned about wiring networks and fiber optic cables. I became proficient in making the most of technology that wasn't there. When I entered the building for the first time, it reminded me of the security at the old company. I wanted to learn and get a better handle on technology to further my career as a technical person rather than just selling the technology.

I ran with a small number of people. I quickly started gaining expertise in new areas—learning how to wire doors for security, run security cables, wire cameras, and build technology from scratch was eye-opening. Then, I got trapped in a situation I could have easily escaped had I not been stuck walking home.

A group of guys from my work decided it was a good idea to go to an apartment after work to party with a group of nurses and have a few beers after our shift. It was out of town from where we normally worked, and I was stuck for the ride. Before I knew it, I was drinking a beer, and the perverse thoughts started running through my head.

I heard a nurse talking about how she had some weed in her room and that we should all get high and smoke some. I refused but held on to my beer as I sat back, wondering what it would be like to get with the nurse with a broken leg.

I learned the next day, while I was climbing a water tower, that the girl I had been hitting on found out I was married. My behavior was due to the side effects of medication my doctor had warned me about. After I came down from the water tower, I was let go from my job. I realized my mistake and knew there was no excuse for my actions. So, I requested my old job back at the computer store.

I stayed with the store for another six months and then had an opportunity from a former installation technician who had left the store. He recommended I apply at the local cable company where he was working. They offered better pay and on-the-job training in customer service over the phone. I thought about it and decided to apply. I was hired immediately, and that was the end of my time in retail sales.

Chapter 4:

2005 - 2006

Returning To Your Vomit

LIKE A DOG THAT RETURNS TO ITS VOMIT, SO IS A FOOL WHO REPEATS HIS FOOLISHNESS.
PROVERBS 26:11 NASB

I left my previous job with the computer superstore. I received confirmation from my new employer that I was welcome to the new place of work at the local cable company. Then, upon going in for my first day, I sat down and listened as they called out my name and pulled me aside to explain that they hadn't hired me. There was a mistake in their procedures, and I was terminated the day after my drug screening came back positive for Meth.

The medication to treat Adult ADD is very close to the street drug speed or methamphetamine. It tests positive in drug screenings for such drugs, and I was completely caught off guard. I had just been put on a drug a couple of years prior, but I had never taken a drug screen since being on it. Surprised by the outcome, I became enraged with anger, and to top it all off, my wife just went into the hospital for appendicitis surgery. My stomach sank as I was without a job on the first day of my new career.

I had taken time off from work to be with her because she had been sick for about two weeks. We thought that it was the flu or another illness, but as her temperature grew and she continued to go to work, I felt that something else was wrong. She waited until she couldn't move anymore. Her appendix burst open inside of her, and she was hurting. Thankfully, my parents came and took her to the hospital. I was finishing my last week at the computer superstore when I got the news. My mom and dad had taken her to see our family doctor, and he said she needed to have emergency surgery right away!

What should have taken about two hours took about 8. The appendix burst and flung fleshy shrapnel in her pelvic area and took out a part of her liver and her colon. They had to stitch it back up and get all of the infectious tissue out of her body. They made a 4-inch incision into her belly and stapled her shut. She was bedridden in the hospital for 11 days. Being the fighter she is, she wanted to return to work practically the same day she got out of surgery. The experience sent my mind racing back to her car accident when she was a teenager. I sat by her side and even slept in the hospital with her. I couldn't believe that I might have lost her if she just waited two more hours.

Sitting in the office behind a closed door with three women, my new employer gave me the talk of a lifetime. They had a plan for such instances, which wasn't for my benefit. I stared them in the face with tears streaming down. Thinking of the pain my wife was in. Knowing I would have to go back to my wife and tell her that I didn't have a job was not something I wanted to do. I had just gotten word that I had been fired the same day I was hired. I did the only thing I knew to do. I fought hard with the people in front of me.

I demanded to know why I wasn't told this sooner. The young lady said the company had sent me a letter stating that I was let go, but the letter came back as "Not at this Address." I explained that I had received a welcome letter and showed them a letter they had sent me at the same address as they had sent the denial letter. The first letter indicated they had hired me. They quickly realized their mistake. The lady claimed that there wasn't anything that they could do. The decision was final, and I would have to prove that I was on the medications. And come back in two weeks to start the next round of training.

I was not about to be out of a job for two more weeks. We had just purchased a house, and my wife was going to have hospital bills. I found out quickly that one of the side effects of the medication I was on was excessive anger and high blood pressure. This wasn't a good combination for me at this point. I demanded that they give me my job.

I was raging mad and threatened to sue them. I asked their corporate office's phone number and told them I would return tomorrow. I went to my doctor's office and got a note explaining my situation. I faxed it to their corporate office and ran around with my head cut off. But I was back the next day, and they couldn't believe it. I was hired and put back into the class but lost a day of training.

The trainer said I wouldn't make it because I lost a day of learning. He claimed that no one ever made it if they didn't get the total training in his classroom. I defied the odds and let the trainer see what I could do. I worked hard to prove my previous employers wrong and was determined to prove this Elvis impersonator wrong.

I watched as the other newly hired team members dropped out of the class. Although I was still attending college, I had completed most of my network training through an online course, so I was in for the long haul.

I met a lot of awesome people at the cable company. A big guy that later became a great friend to this day. He was a survivor of a serious accident. He was thrown from a moving van and landed in a ditch, breaking a lot of his body. He claimed that God saved his life. I met a former trucker turned computer technical genius. She was like my best friend during the hard times at the beginning. I helped her out a lot, and she showed me many things about how to be loving toward others. I don't know if she was a Christian, but she had a lot of questions about faith. We all worked nights and weekends together. Due to the turnover rate, we all moved up in the company quickly.

I moved up to the business support role during my first year there. I started my new role with a phobia towards anything professional business-related due to my mistakes with the "Don't think like the rest of the world company." My previous employer told me I needed more business sense, and the fear kept creeping into my mind that I would mess it up again. "You're not technical! So stop trying to be technical! You don't know business or how to work a business!" I calmed most of those voices with my new business degree in computer technology. I was out to prove the voices wrong.

My old manager claimed that I wasn't a good problem solver. He called me an ADD boy and made me wear a shirt that stated that fact. Everything cruel people in this world had said about me was wrong. I was winning the war against those voices and had something to prove.

The medications seemed to be helping me think better and faster on my feet. They made me a heavy thinker and a problem solver, giving me a sense of purpose and allowing me to do more with my life. The medications seemed to help me adapt to my surroundings faster. But there was a negative side to this medication. One that was about to drag me down a deep, dark hole of despair and turmoil.

The medication helped me to stay focused on whatever I was focused on for hours at a time. The medication was causing me to do some crazy things. The medication would keep me focused on whatever task was before me. It helped to hold my concentration for hours at a time. The problem was that my focus after work was on Internet-related things. I was watching pornography when I got home for hours. I was neglecting my wife.

I watched pornography 8 hours a day at times. I concentrated on chatting with women to feel more attractive. The medications built up my confidence in my intellect but turned me into a jerk. I would accuse my wife of being mean and unloving; all the while, I was one foot out the door with other women.

I chatted with girls online and became more assertive in my actions. I had many women conversing with me for hours a night. This was all during my first few years at the cable company. I would stay up until 5 AM. It was as if I couldn't stop myself. My mind kept focusing on the sexual thoughts and fantasies. I was living a double life. The pornography kept getting weirder. The extreme wasn't extreme enough to keep my interest.

I would get on Yahoo Messenger and share pictures of myself with several women. It was exciting and unbearable at the same time. My shame grew all the more as I couldn't stop trying to be more attractive and get my fix of sex. One woman in particular was a beautiful redhead. I remembered it vaguely, but I remembered the woman's face and name. I even tried stalking her online. I became obsessed with her so much that it scared me to see how far I was going down a dark path.

I searched for her at my workplace and found her information. I could have called and met her in person, but I couldn't get her out of my mind. I couldn't tell what stopped me other than the grace of God.

I found a group of men who wanted to help me escape this life, but I didn't want the help. I went to a meeting and left, thinking that it wasn't for me. I wasn't the problem. The world was the problem. My wife was the problem. My family, my abuse, and my life were the problem. I wasn't the problem. I was bound and determined to prove the world wrong.

I was so wrapped up in a world that I made up that I didn't see my marriage and my life around me going up in flames. God gave my wife a lot of patience; otherwise, I knew she should have divorced me then. She has been the most patient and perfectly beautiful woman in the world to me. I don't understand how she could have stood by me for so long, but I know God had a plan.

Sex was all that I seemed to have on my mind all of the time that I was on the medication. When it wore off, I crashed hard and went even more stir-crazy. From what I could remember, my moods were all over the place. I thought I was being rational and everyone else was crazy. My logic was sound, and I felt I was doing things all guys did in their relationships. That was what the pornography sites were teaching me. I was trying to live out the fantasy life of those videos, and I couldn't stop looking at them or thinking about them.

I looked like a kind and gentle human to the outside world. But behind closed doors, I was a scoundrel and monster. I would play Dungeons and Dragons with my friends in our basement. I remember several nights we would be playing, the medication would wear off, and I would fall asleep in front of everyone playing. This was another side-effect of the medication for ADD. It was like I had narcolepsy. I couldn't control it, and it made me feel horrible when someone would wake me up for my turn to play.

My friends thought I was bored with them and the game, but that wasn't the case. I tried to force myself to stay awake and be a good host, but the more I struggled, the worse my tiredness became. It didn't help that we were wasted from shots of 151 and beer.

One night, we were so drunk that one of my friends tripped over his own feet, face-planted on the floor, and vomited his pizza onto the carpet. I went to bed, and my wife had to stay up to clean up the mess. I heard about it the next morning. Months later, mold still lingered in the carpet where he landed. I was focused on myself, and that was all that mattered.

One evening, a girl from my high school days found me online in a chat room. We started talking about our pasts and how we were both abused growing up. We talked for what seemed like hours, and she had been in a broken relationship and marriage. I claimed the same thing but only wanted to say the right words to get in bed with her.

We discussed many things, including hidden secrets like the nurse incident that resulted in my firing a few years back. We also spoke about life in general. She was the youth pastor at my old church, and I knew she was a terrible example for the children she was teaching. She was also the Boy Scout troop den leader, so I followed her to the church to closely monitor what she was doing.

The church was two houses away from my family home. She became friends with my wife for a short time. She came to our home on a couple of occasions. She would bring along her boyfriend, whom she was with while married to another man. She even made sexual advances toward my wife, which seemed normal to me at the time. In my head, I wanted more than one girl at a time, and this was the perfect opportunity. It was what I constantly saw in the videos I watched online. I could see the fantasy play out in my mind. I kept following her to the church. And I was persistent in my actions due to the medication keeping my focus.

At that time, the church pastor was getting a divorce from his wife. He wasn’t in a position to give me a lesson on marriage, so I didn't know what to think about it. He was a great person, and he married my wife and me. I didn't realize how much that divorce would affect the church.

I knew the people at the church were a bunch of hypocrites, and they wanted him gone. The church members claimed to be one thing and did another, much like the youth leader, the girl I had been chasing down and chatting with online. Mostly, they were as evil as I was, but they tried to hide it behind fancy clothes and greeted people with a smile. I had never claimed to be a Christian except when it pertained to impressing the girls.

In the back of my mind, I wanted to call them all out, but at the same time, all I could think about was being with her and my secrets being found out. I couldn't separate the two. I decided to get more involved with the church and be around her to monitor her actions. Then God intervened.

A new pastor was assigned to the church, which the congregation said they wanted. The church claimed they wanted a Spanish-speaking pastor. They didn’t know the neighborhood. We were a poor, white-dominated area with only a few Spanish-speaking neighbors. I felt like they wanted a pastor who would be easy to push around, so the committee took a vote for the qualities they said they wanted, and off they went.

I didn't know why they wanted a Spanish-speaking pastor or a woman. I think they thought she would be a pushover. I didn't know where Honduras was, but I knew it was a Spanish-speaking country. I was returning to the church again after several years, but I felt like something was guiding me back there after being absent for so long. God seemed to be calling me back there for some reason. I believed this was it.

I had grown up in this church with another young woman I thought wasn't my friend then. She had a horrible attitude and a weird husband who was all about God, or so he claimed. I kept my distance from them for a while.

He claimed that he had found Jesus early on in his life. He was all about having Jesus in his life daily. He wanted to become a pastor. He tried to help others fight the battle of addiction. I just thought that he was a crazy nutjob. But then again, I felt that going to church was about being good and being a better person or just chasing after sex and women. After all, all of the crazy women went to church. That was my experience, at least.

I didn't have a clue what I was doing. I saw their happy family. They were creating something beautiful, and I was thinking of ways to tear it down. I thought they were fake, obscure, and out of touch. I listened to the opinion of the girl I had been chasing after about their lifestyle instead of getting to know them personally. I found out that she was possibly sleeping with random kids in her youth group and taking them out for joy rides in her jeep. I was so messed up that my moral compass was not even existent at this point.

Might As Well Face it!

I was asked to come to church on the Sunday when the new pastor was introduced to the congregation. I wanted to see who they had picked. I knew what this congregation could do to anyone with a weak demeanor. If she were out of touch with their schemes, they would eat someone like her up, chew her up, and spit her out.

The former youth leader, who taught me about Christ when I was younger, pulled me aside and asked me to hold a massive globe and stand right here. A pre-typed speech on the side said, "We give you this globe as a piece offering of love and worldly compassion for our neighbors." I stood in line to welcome the new pastor with theatrical precision and a quaint look of hospitality and love.

It was the same loving welcome you would get from being in a cage with many hungry lions, hoping they don't see you in the corner cowering. Everyone in the church sat two pews away from the new pastor's family in every direction. Vicious vipers surrounded the new Pastor's family, and they looked like food for the prey until she stood up and spoke.

At that moment, God spoke to my heart and reminded me of a high school friend. A thought came to my mind as I stood there holding the globe. The high school girl I was friends with spoke fluent Spanish. A time that we were together walking around her neighborhood came ringing back into my mind. I was reminded of the story of when we walked down a dark street on the city's north side. I was scared of the people I saw. People who were drug users, homeless, and worn down buildings all around us. I quietly spoke up to my friend, voiced my opinion, and asked, "How are you not scared to walk down these streets?" And she replied, "Now you know how I feel walking down your streets when I come to see you."

Then, something came into my heart as the new pastor spoke up. I don't remember what she said, but I remember that she was a refugee from a war-torn country who wanted to share the love of Jesus with us. Just as quickly, she sat back down with her family. I heard a love that I had never heard before that day. I could understand her completely, but everyone else had difficulty understanding her.

Her words had power as she spoke, but all I could remember were the words of my friend penetrating my heart as I stared at this pastor's family. The pastor's daughter was beautiful and sweet. Her husband was quiet yet very rugged and very laid-back. Their lives had a history of war and neglect. It was a story that needed to be told. I wanted to know more about them. It was almost like they knew the abuse I grew up with. Then, I heard God speak for the first time. "Help her rebuild my church."

Then, all the guilty thoughts and sinful past mistakes rushed in to silence the voice. Being on this so-called medication for ADD was causing me to think irrationally. My mind went right back to the women. I continued to see women online and dreamed of being with the pastor's daughter in the back of my mind.

I didn't want to think of either the pastor or her daughter that way, but my mind couldn't stop. It was spiraling out of control, and I felt horrible about all of those thoughts. But they wouldn’t stop attacking my mind. I kept it all hidden in my head and didn't want to address the issues with anyone. So I kept them to myself. I thought, “If they knew what I was thinking or who I was, they would kick me out the first chance they got!”

As the pastor approached me and thanked me for the warm welcome, I had to tell her about the congregation and their way of dealing with people. I told her about God’s voice and how he wanted me to help her rebuild His church. I had to tell her the congregation didn't want her there and were all doing this to make a statement that they would do anything to keep their social club going. New faces, such as the Hispanic community, meant more money for the church to stay open, but they didn't want Spanish-speaking men and women in the church.

The congregation wanted to look good before the general conference and played nice to their faces. I knew the congregation’s schemes from previous pastors. After the pastor who married my wife and I left due to the divorce and being stomped on for all of those years, it was a new playing field for them, and they all knew it. I asked the pastor from Honduras to sit down and talk with me about the concerns I had for her safety, and I shared some of my past with her. I explained that many people here, including the youth leader, are not here to worship. They were there for social benefits and to occasionally serve others. They were not genuine about their faith life, but something in my heart wanted to change. I tried to get closer to God. I wanted to see what this pastor had to offer. Her messages pulled me in.

Over the next several weeks, I felt she was talking directly to me. She spoke words that I had never heard before in my entire life. The love in her words brought comfort and conviction to my heart. She spoke with authority and experience, as though she had a real relationship with a loving God I had never known a person could have.

It wasn't the same Jesus I had learned about in Sunday school from the lady who embarrassed me by giving me the huge globe. This was a pastor who had a real relationship with a heavenly Father. This was someone who knew Jesus personally. She had power in her words and took the room by storm when she spoke. Jesus was flowing through her with every word. I had never seen a pastor like this before. She made me want to know more about this person she passionately spoke about every Sunday from the pulpit. But I also wanted to hold on to my old ways.

The God she was talking about couldn't exist, could He? Could a God like that be forgiving to a person like me? I was a child molester by the world's standards. I had sex with my 6-year-old nephew when I was 12, and coming out about that just about ruined my life. A god that could forgive that wasn't a god that I had ever heard of. How could God, a good judge, love a person like me so much, and He wanted to bring me back from these sickening mistakes? This was not a god of the world.

And looking at all of the pornography that I had seen, and all of the drugs, all of the sinful acts that I had done against women all of my life, how could God love me as she proudly stated every Sunday in her sermons? I listened to her and started to feel a change in my heart. It came on slowly at first, but a change nonetheless.

The change wasn't magical or demanding of me. I slowly and steadily progressed and learned more daily. I wanted to give this God thing more of my time. I started to read about this God she was talking about. I even bought a bible that I could read that wasn't a King James Bible. I had forgotten who I thought people saw me as for a short time. I was learning about how Jesus died for me. He took me to the cross and asked me to lay my past abuse, my sinful nature, and all of the problems I had brought throughout the years and lay them down so He could take them away.

I didn't want to believe it at first. Then I saw something I never thought possible. I saw the chaos and damage I was causing. The rapture at my feet, my past haunting me, pulling me back into the world I had created, full of filthy rags and shame. The shame was unbearable if I were to walk away from Jesus now. Where would I go? How could I still be on the fence at this point?

I continued to listen to the pastor, but I also continued to do the same things I had been doing before. I looked at child pornography. I looked at the worst parts of pornography on the Internet. The desires continued to get worse. I felt like I was being drawn away from what this pastor was saying to me. I was being pulled in two different directions constantly. A familiar but pain-filled direction of sin and another direction under the care of a living, breathing, life-giving God who died on the cross to free me from my sin. Sin was tearing me apart and trying to consume me more and more. “Lord, give me a reason to break free from all this!”

One night, while chatting with a girl online, I heard a convulsing body shaking in our bedroom. It was my wife. The time was about 2 AM, and I stared at the computer for about ten more seconds to ensure I had turned everything off. Then I ran in and called 911.

I watched as my wife convulsed terribly for about 10 minutes while I waited for the ambulance to arrive. I tried holding her down, but the shaking didn't stop. I wanted to keep her from biting her tongue as she foamed at the mouth. My heart raced as I looked at the woman I had loved for so many years, flailing around helplessly on our bed.

Finally, the paramedics arrived, and I shut down the computer. They stabilized her body and made sure she was coherent. They asked if she wanted to go to the hospital in the ambulance or in a car with me. I wasn't sure what to do, so I asked my parents to take both of us to the hospital. She was exhausted by the event.

I was feeling nauseous and wanting to vomit, thinking about how quickly my actions could have set me down a different path. But then I was kicked right in the gut when I heard the doctor speak about her condition. He said that the seizures could have been caused by excessive exhaustion and tiredness from a lack of sleep.

My wife had been suffering from epileptic seizures throughout her childhood and a part of her teenage life. She hadn't had a seizure since she was 14 years old. She was now 26 years old. I accepted her health issues as she had accepted mine. At that moment, I felt like I wanted out of the whole marriage, but something told me I was wrong about it and that God would show me something different. God spoke into my heart and told me that my actions were at fault for this. And that I had better stay around, repent, and make things right.

She loved me so much that she would stay up for hours after I got off work to wait for me to get to bed. She knew I was watching pornography. She knew what I was doing behind closed doors but loved me anyway. I do know that something in my heart started to change that night. I broke down and cried excessively. I had to ask God why he had to hurt her and not me. Why did she have to have a seizure and be hurt instead of me? I was the terrible person in this! Not her!

Then, I couldn't forget the whole incident for weeks. I waited on her hand and foot, going to bed with her every night for several months. I cleared out my history, closed my accounts, and tried to return my life to normal.

One night, about two months after the seizure, I couldn't sleep. I wanted to look at pornography, but I couldn't do it. I made it to the office and turned on the computer only to remember her shaking body and the pain she was in. I went out of my office back into the bedroom and started crying in my pillow. I cried so hard that it woke her up. She asked me what was wrong, but I didn't want to say anything. Deep under my emotions was a tidal wave of shame about to unleash a change in my soul and crush my life as I knew it forever.

I couldn't sleep because I had kept a massive secret from everyone for years. I had made advances towards other women, including her friends, while we were still dating in high school. My cousins and my brother molested me for years, and so many people in school and throughout my entire life abused me. All of the sins that were bottled up came pouring out that night.

We sat up most of the night and talked about it all. She kept trying to get me to sleep, and I wanted to, but I was spewing out more and more sins, and it spiraled out of control. The thoughts kept coming. I couldn't hold any of it back any longer. It was like projectile vomit all over the room.

Finally, I calmed down enough while she held onto my nearly lifeless body, calmed me down with affection, and told me she loved me so much. She suggested we talk to the doctor about seeing a counselor about all of it and find out why I was acting the way I was. So, I made an appointment to see a therapist.

Chapter 5:

2006 - 2007

Going through Hell Backwards

THEREFORE, CONFESS YOUR SINS TO ONE ANOTHER AND PRAY FOR ONE ANOTHER SO THAT YOU MAY BE HEALED. WHEN IT IS BROUGHT ABOUT, A RIGHTEOUS PERSON'S PRAYER CAN ACCOMPLISH MUCH. JAMES 5:16 NASB

Often, when we give our lives over to the care of Christ, we are instantly attacked. This was the case for my life. Having started to give God my all, Satan came into attack. My wife's grandmother was hit with a sudden aneurysm and died from a blood clot in the brain. It was something that her grandparents prayed for. They agreed and made a covenant promise with God that she should go home first, but in her given the time. Was this something that God would grant? It seemed like asking to die in a certain order was not something God would want us to pray about. In their eyes, it was a God-given gift that she went home to be with Christ first. My question was how God did this and worked miracles. It seemed senseless to pray for such a thing, but it happened the way they had prayed. She died peacefully in her sleep. Her grandfather was sad for a time seeing the love of his life die, but he knew something that I had never known. He knew who he served, and that one was God.

After her death, I started seeking help with all of my problems. At first, the therapist was a great help. She showed me many ways to deal with my past trauma and helped me get past the abuse I endured. But when she heard that I had sexually abused my nephew when I was 12 years old, she suggested that I be locked up and throw away the key. I join a 12-step group for people with sexual addictions. So I went for a couple of weeks and then thought that it wasn't for me after she said I should be locked up. I didn't want to go back to her again. I could beat the problems on my own and skip the therapy. "Who was this lady to say I was crazy and needed to be locked up?" I thought to myself. If I continued attending church, that would be my therapy.

The girl I had been going to see at church was gone for the summer with the Boy Scouts troop. She had taken the whole summer off from being a youth leader. The pastor took notice and wondered why we were stopping the youth program over the summer months. The girl left about eight young women and a couple of young boys with nothing to do for the summer because they weren't a part of the scouting group.

Having a keen eye for talent, the pastor asked if I would want to help take on the youth group. The pastor saw something in me with these young men and women. I didn't see it then, but they looked up to me, and I had a way with children. Not abusively, but I could talk to them on their level, and they respected me as someone who paid attention to their needs. With the help of my wife and the other couple that the youth leader disliked, the pastor asked me to lead the youth group that was left to lead for the summer. We decided to have a vacation bible school program and youth group during her absence. Initially, I declined because I knew about my background, but the pastor insisted I lead it. And so I became the youth leader that summer.

I didn't know much about the Bible or God, but I did know about kids and what they were into. At the time, I had every video game system imaginable. I could relate to the kids on their level because I was still a kid at heart. I could teach them computer skills, play video games, and get to know them better.

While teaching the youth, the pastor helped me learn the Bible and what it meant to have a real relationship with Jesus. My wife and I, along with the other couple, were a powerhouse team, and we grew the youth group almost overnight to about sixty youth. We got new teen kids into the church youth group almost daily that summer, but word traveled quickly to the old youth leader that things were changing in her absence.

She found me online one night as I tried slipping back into my old behaviors, and I sparingly confided in her some of the plans we had made to bring more youth to the church, thinking that she would enjoy how much we had grown the program. To my dismay, she came back that summer enraged with jealousy. She hated the other couple we had grown the youth group with, and she spewed evil thoughts over everything we had built up. She came out about what I had told her in confidence about my past. I knew it would be a horrible chain of events, as did the pastor, but we didn't know what chaos she had planned. The chaos she did have planned was to destroy what we had built.

I tried explaining to the old youth pastor that I didn't want to lead the group, but the new pastor asked me to lead as she saw I had the children's attention. The pastor could see that I was good at leading children, and so were my friends. I knew the old youth pastor loved leading kids, and I was in her way of keeping that dream alive. She then proceeded to threaten me further by exposing my past sexual behavior. She thought that bringing my darkness into the light of day would expose me and cause me to lose control of the situation. My only thought was, “How could this be a good thing, God?”

I knew she was doing the same things behind closed doors, and I wasn’t the only one guilty of those sinful acts. I wanted to say more about her part, but God called me to avoid mentioning it. So, I remained silent to save face in front of the church.

One day, the district superintendent emailed me asking for my story about the situation. At that moment, I knew my past was on trial. I was going to be hanged and nailed to the cross like Jesus. I couldn't keep it hidden any longer. I had to tell the world my story about how Jesus changed my life. I didn't want to be the person I was before. I wrote a letter explaining the situation, confessing my part and telling the superintendent what I knew of the old youth leader’s side, which surprised the old youth leader. The superintendent said I needed to step down as youth leader and give it to the other couple leading beside me. He said he would investigate my side of the story and that the Scouting troop would no longer meet at the church.

I explained that I wanted to avoid the youth leadership role in the first place. However, the youth felt rejected by not being in the scouts. They felt left behind, and I wanted to make sure they saw the love of Jesus that I saw. I stepped down that day and asked that the Scouts be investigated for the youth leader's actions and be disbanded until further notice.

I learned that several of the scout leaders in the group were having sexual parties. My wife was invited to a couple of those parties, but she refused to tell me because of my mental capacity for sexual exploits and further corrupting my captive mindset. She explained it to me later after I made the claims about what I knew, and we gave that information to the church leadership committee. I didn't want it to blow up heavily, but God knew what he was doing. Sin has a way of destroying many things all at once.

As I grew in my relationship with Jesus through the pastor's help, I learned more about myself and how I treated others in the past was wrong. I decided to study to become a pastor with my new mentor's assistance. I wanted to change my life, but I had to face a lot of demons. That included my past abuse, my sexual escapades with other women online, and the abuse of my nephew.

I remembered being sexual towards my wife's sister at some point but stopping myself. I remember trying to throw myself at any person attracted to me. On the superintendent's and my pastor's advice, I was asked to seek counseling again and possibly return to sex addiction meetings. I needed to talk to someone I could confide in who knew what I was going through.

That's when I met the Christian therapist who helped me write my story. This is where my story takes a turn for the worse, if you can believe it. It's not that therapy isn't good for healing or that being a Christian doesn't fix your life for the better… I am a Christian today because of the people who have come into my life, but the things I had to endure to get to this point were something no one else should face alone, and I promise there is hope on the other side.

Just a bit of a warning. The rest of the story is where I can't remember much due to medications the doctors put me on, and I am referring to journals that I had put into practice during this time. This is also how I found out who I was in Christ and how He wanted me to experience this to share with the world why we need to learn to fight these battles of depression, anxiety, and ADD without the use of medications and get back to the world God created us for and not the world we see on television and Facebook.

This journal is a reflection on who I was while on three different medications and various results as I progressed down a road that led to human trafficking and the buying of girls online. This is also the reason God put it on my heart to help lead the charge to stop this form of slavery and speak up for the men and women who are still trapped in it.

Once the cat of my escapades was out of the bag and I was shown grace by my pastor and the Superintendent of the church conference, I was asked to resign as the youth director and follow my mentor's lead. I took on other leadership roles in the church and had several opportunities to study under the pastor. Many members left the church for a time due to the scandal. We had to move on. It became prevalent that what I had spoken up about the first day the pastor had arrived was true, and I needed to be on guard now.

I returned to get help with my sexual thoughts through counseling and a support group of men and women who were dealing with the same thoughts and problems I was facing. I was breaking down further as I was going to these meetings and starting counseling. I would tell the truth about my feelings and actions, but I wasn't about to share what I had done in the past with anyone else. The hurt was too much to bear.

However, God seemed to know my heart and kept working on me through my pastor friends. The pastor was being shot at by many of the remaining members of the congregation due to their loyalty to their friends who had left the church. The scout group had disbanded and were not welcome back to the church due to their tactics of demanding that they were superior to the church. There was a full-on investigation into what was happening to the children of the group, and threats were made to the pastor because of all of it. Eventually, the waters settled for a time.

We all got back to worshiping and fellowshiping. The pastor showed me what it was to be loved at this point. I saw God in a different light and started to work more in the church. We let go of the janitor and took care of the facilities ourselves. We were told that there was money to reseed the yard of the church and that it would cost several thousands of dollars by the remaining members. We asked to see their books, but they refused to show them. They were holding back thousands of dollars in funds and using it for personal use. We ended up starting over with just a few members. God had given us the church and told us to take care of it for a time. Then, new members started flowing in. The youth group was beginning to grow, and new people were coming back for the first time in years. But like anything when building God's kingdom, Satan was waiting to pounce on the few of us, starting an uprising.

For about two years, we worked hard to bring the church around to God and his word. At that time, I worked harder than ever to learn what God wanted for my life. I asked God to show me what he wanted me to do. He showed me in several ways. He asked me to continue to clean up the church by peering into people's hearts and seeing their motives. Before I looked into other people's lives, he asked me to search my heart for his love and blessings on things in my life. He told me to follow him and do the work even if I didn't have help. He told me that he would help me when I needed it. How did he do that? Here's how.

One day, after a meeting with the district superintendent, our pastor found out that the chairman of the treasury was scheming and stealing money. She confronted him in front of the church body, and he was pulled down from his position. The next day, the chairperson's uncle came into the pastor's office full of anger and rage and beat on the pastor's door. She felt threatened by his actions and asked to be moved due to her past persecution from similar situations. It was a huge mess, and I was now fighting for her to stay, but her mind had been made up. God was calling her to continue to lead me, but she would be doing it from within the security of her home and during worship services.

I had started following the pastor and being around her more than anything else. My wife and I discussed what we would do if she left the church and moved. We decided to continue worshipping there briefly, but that was cut short when others started returning. So, we went with my mentor to a new church plant in a small town.

Before my wife and I left the church, I had an experience beyond words that would change my life forever. I met Jesus Christ face to face. It seemed weird then, but the more I reflected on that day, the more I knew it was him.

Chapter 6:

2007 - 2008

Face to Face With Jesus Christ

It happened that while Jesus was praying in a certain place, after He had finished, one of His disciples said to Him, "Lord, teach us to pray just as John also taught his disciples." Luke 11:1 NASB

The world was struggling to make ends meet. My wife and I were no exception, facing problems with the housing market and debt. We tried many things. We went to various debt counselors who offered guidance, but we found out they wanted more money to help us get out of our debt. We became skeptical of asking for help after we received "Help" from the mortgage company through which we refinanced our home.

The refinancing terms were way better than our contract when we originally purchased the house, but the broker lied about the home's assessment value to get us more money. We decided not to take them up on their offer, only to find ourselves in court over what they claimed were signed documents but looked like forged records. We found ourselves in even deeper debt after that.

One evening, a debt collector came knocking on our door for my vehicle. They said they could take it now or leave me stranded in some random parking lot when I wasn't looking. I handed over my vehicle reluctantly and asked how we could get it back and settle the debt. They said they would be in contact soon and that I needed to pay them back the full amount of the car I owed due to my delinquent payments.

We also got behind on our house payment, so we signed up for a new O'Bama loan through another bank, only to find out it wasn't what we had hoped for. We fought with them for months to get things straightened out, but it only worsened. Eventually, we found a program that would assist with our home payments, but it required us to be delinquent for about six months before we could qualify. The delinquency led to our home being in foreclosure status. We were in this situation because we followed the advice of self-serving individuals who offered only empty words and no real support.

We were left with one option for a vehicle. We had to borrow a vehicle from my aunt so that I could commute to work temporarily. We needed time to gather the funds to buy a new vehicle and pay off our existing debts. Unfortunately, our financial situation seemed to spiral out of control beyond recovery.

One evening in the winter, I found myself staring at a dead van at a gas station on my way home from work. It was the van I had borrowed from my aunt. I had pulled into the gas station parking lot to fill it up. I finished adding fuel to the van and returned to start it up again. The battery was dead. The van's hood was frozen shut from ice, so I couldn't get into the battery area to charge it. So, I began to pray.

That wasn't the first time the van broke down on me. Just weeks before, I had been asked to give a sermon at the church. The pastor was on sabbatical, and I was gaining knowledge as a future pastor. I thought I did well in giving the sermon. The congregation was pleased, and I had to rush out to get to work. Shaking everyone's hand, saying good day to them, and leaving for work, I rushed home to get ready.

I hopped into my aunt's van and started up the street, only to have the van die at the end of the road at a T-intersection. Tears rolling down my face, ashamed of being stuck, I called my wife and asked her to pick me up so I could get to work. Then, rescue came from the church members—only they drove past.

One after the next drove by in disgust. Even with my tear-filled eyes, I could see the look on their faces. "Was this person's van broken down? We have places to get to!" The sounds of voices were in my mind as they stared with disgusted looks, only to see it was me and continue past to move on with their day.

The older people I had known for years were the first to go past. Then, the people who said they cared about me shook my hand and told me they loved me. Then, the former youth leaders who trained me as a youth. Finally, God came by to teach me a lesson. I began to pray for the van to start. After my old youth leaders drove past, the van started back up.

They had all seen me crying and worried, and just minutes before that time, they had seen me give a sermon on helping others. The message must not have stuck. It was as if God was showing me who they were. God showed up and started the van without effort.

God also wanted me to see they were not who I thought they were. He wanted me to see that the church was full of hypocrites. I am a hypocrite as well, at times. The difference is in how we love others. They were not loving others by passing me by, knowing someone was stuck, and staring them in the face. They knew who I was and wouldn't help me. I could only think about the "Good Samaritan" story in scripture. And how only God could bring me out of my situation.

I was stuck at the gas station, praying for another miracle in the cold dead of winter. I couldn't get the van to start. It seemed like a dead battery. I released the hood latch and jumped out of the van to assess the situation. The hood was frozen shut from the ice storm. I pounded and pressed the hood, but it wouldn't budge. Finally, with a huge push, the ice broke loose, and an older man came out of nowhere; we scared each other as the hood popped open. We both screamed with high-pitched noises from our lips.

After dying from heart attacks and coming back down into our bodies, the older gentleman asked if I could use some help. He said it looked like I could use a lot of help. I said I was unsure what was happening with this van, but it constantly died at random spots, and I just wanted to get home. He offered to jump my van and even offered to follow me home. I told him he didn't have to go that far, but. I could use a jump. His wife brought the car over, and they helped me start the van. I headed home quickly, praying the van wouldn't stop again. I kept thinking, did God send the angels to help me?

God has always shown up in times of need, but these experiences were beyond supernatural; it felt like several planned events took me down a path I wasn't following. The next event changed my whole life. It was when I experienced God face to face. Given the times I had little to go on for money, given our financial situation, this was a miracle.

I had been working for the cable company for five years and was recently promoted to the network administrator of the Master headend of the North Division. One evening, I came into work to see my Divisional Manager in the control room. I was excited to see him working hard and helping with the business. Uncertain why he was in the building, I went in to see if I could help him with anything, as he rarely got his hands dirty.

As I drew closer to his presence, I noticed he was in a horrible mood. His face was red with blood boiling, which made me less than excited that he was there. He blew up with anger at everyone, including me. He demanded to know why I didn't know the entire system yet. I explained that I had yet to be taught a part of the system that had given them trouble that day. It had been a specific person's job to manage the set-top-box hardware, and I was a networking person, but he didn't want to hear any of it.

He yelled commands at all of us and called the manufacturer's help desk to fix the issue. I did everything he commanded me to do. For the first time, I saw a manager I worked for struggling to control the situation. He allowed his anger to spill over to the rest of his employees. Then he proceeded to yell at me in anger and say that I was worthless. I was no good to him if I didn't know all the systems. He then started calling everyone profane names.

Given his position in the cable company, his actions surprised me. He seemed angry at the whole operation—so bitterly angry that it felt like a life-or-death situation. I tried to dismiss it as spur-of-the-moment aggression, but then he came at me directly and told me how worthless I was again and that I needed to catch up on training or I would be fired. I excused myself and went to the break room to cool down.

I had seen anger like this in my father at times, and I had seen it when my brother abused me. I knew that whenever I saw that kind of aggression, my mind would lock up, and I couldn't move or think. With tears rolling down my face, I began to pray. "Lord, help me get out of this situation! Help me to find another more fitting job!" I didn't need another financial disaster to hit in my life. His actions made me question why I took on the role. The job consisted of watching pornography and other channels that I would have never watched before the role. It consisted of quality-checking every channel the cable company offered. It allowed me to see the side of the cable company most people never see. My role had so much control that I could have changed every channel to a kid's television show and could have caused a whole global catastrophe for the cable television network. I had power that I didn't want, but I knew I had it to control. But at that moment in that prayer, all I wanted was to be out of that situation at that very moment. All the abuse I endured and all of the trauma peered into my soul, and I was a child crying in a corner of the house all over again, hoping someone would rescue me.

I was hurt because I worked hard to train my mind for the role. I had gone back to school to get my degree. I endured long hours to prove I was good enough of a technical person to beat out my old employer at the "Don't Think Like the Rest of the World" company. I had tried to be perfect in the role, but I knew I had more to learn. At that very moment, I knew God had other plans for me. Little did I know that this prayer I prayed in the breakroom of a trailer at the cable company would set me down a course to follow God where He wanted me to go.

I finished the prayer, and just as I said, "Amen," my cell phone rang. I received a call from an IT recruiter. I had not applied for a job in over four years. How did this recruiter get my résumé? The situation scared me at first. Like in the Truman Show, it was as if some strange recruiter was spying on me. "Hello! You don't know me, but I am a recruiter from a recruiting company, and I came across your resume and thought you would be a good fit for a role I am having a hard time filling." He claimed with excitement. " "Would you be interested?"

All I could think about was the timing of his call and what I had just prayed for. Did God answer my prayer right then and there? I said to the recruiter, "You know, normally I would have just let your call go to voicemail, but you called me at a weirdly good time, and my boss just went off on a tangent, and I went into the breakroom to cry, and I asked God to help me get out of my current situation, then you called me when I got done praying. But, yes, I am looking at a new opportunity if you have one open," I said with tear-filled enthusiasm.

I listened to the recruiter describe the job he was promoting, and he asked me some questions about the role I was currently in. I didn't want to say too much with the irate manager breathing down my neck, but I was delighted at the opportunity to leave such a hostile situation. The new role involved doing the same work as the role at the cable company, and it was about three times the pay. We scheduled time to have an "over-the-phone" interview in a week, and I was blown away at the thought of how quickly God seemed to move. Just a few days before this occurred, the manager, who was now blowing up at me, said he wouldn't give me a pay raise unless I became network-certified, as if my college degree wasn't good enough.

A week had passed, and the recruiter called me back at the designated time. I had taken the call at work while no one else was around. I walked into the server room where I could keep my thoughts collected, and we conducted my interview secretly. The role I was interviewing for seemed like a dream come true. I would perform network administration duties for a large company in the city's downtown area. It would be a nine-to-five shift with benefits. It offered retirement benefits and healthcare benefits. I was ready to jump at the opportunity right then.

After speaking with him over the phone, he said the company wanted a second interview with me. They wanted to interview me in greater detail to ensure I was the right fit for the role. The second interview was a two-hour interview with even more technical questions. Thankfully, I had just finished my degree in networking, and I had been working at the cable company long enough that it was all fresh in my mind. I answered their questions in great detail, and they loved every answer. I had all of the qualifications, but they had one other person they wanted to interview. So I waited patiently for their reply.

A week later, I received a call from the recruiter saying that someone else had been offered the role. They had given it over to the other person who had interviewed after me. He was more qualified and had more experience in the field. I was feeling a little down. I was sure God had given me this opportunity to take on a new role. The recruiter said he would keep my contact information and call me if anything else came up. I was a little depressed about not getting the role, but I knew I still had a job at the cable company.

About a week had passed, and I was resting at home, waiting to go to work that evening. I received a call from the recruiter who originally called me for the job opportunity. "Had he found something else already?" I thought. He asked if I was still interested in the role. The previous candidate decided to pursue a different opportunity. Excited about the opportunity to start a new career, I said, "Yes! I was still interested." I told the recruiter I could start in two weeks to give my current employer time to find a replacement. The recruiter said he would relay the message and get back to me to confirm the offer. He said, "You still wanted $20 per hour, Right?" "Sure!" "Yes!" "That's what we agreed on!" I said with excitement. He said, "Give me about 10 minutes to review the details with the hiring company, and I will get back to you once we have gone over all the details."

After I got off the phone with the recruiter, I waited eagerly for the return call. To my surprise, a call came back quicker than the original 10 minutes had been offered. Was it more bad news? Did they want more details? Did they give the job to someone else? Upon looking at the caller ID, I saw a call from the church secretary. Should I answer it knowing the recruiter would call back at any moment? Figuring it was something minor, I answered the call; maybe it was the recruiter, and the caller ID was broken.

The voice on the other end of the call was desperate and crying for help. The church secretary called me to report that a man had walked into the church and asked to spend the night there. Some random homeless guy had tricked his way into the church building, hoping to get a free place to stay the night. The man claimed to be an Evangelist preaching on street corners, delivering his message from the Book of Revelations.

The stranger had been staying in shelters around town but found sleeping difficult, with sick people coughing and sneezing around him. The noise kept him up at night, so he left, hoping a church would put him up for a night. He was worried about catching a cold, so he came to the church hoping to find shelter. The situation was urgent, and the secretary needed someone to help decide what to do next. I inquired the secretary of the pastor's whereabouts, and the secretary informed me that the pastor was busy with her schoolwork and couldn't be disturbed. I offered to come over and talk with the man who wanted to stay the night in the church. I told the secretary I was waiting for an important phone call and couldn't be out very long. She assured me it wouldn't take much time, but she couldn't handle him alone. She was scared of the situation and didn't know what to do.

Upon entering the church, I asked the secretary if she knew the man's name and what she wanted me to do for him. She said she didn't know his name, but he was in the Narthex. She hadn't asked his name or gotten too personal with him. She just wanted him gone as he smelled like a homeless person and even looked the part. He wore heavy layers of tattered clothing, glasses, a long beard, and long black hair. He had a heavy bag of what looked like books with him for studying. He smelled like he hadn't showered in several weeks. And I walked into where he was looking around and praying for an opportunity to stay somewhere warm and undisturbed for a night. So I asked him his name to get to know him better. He muttered something I couldn't quite comprehend under his breath, and then I introduced myself and our church secretary.

He told me the same story, asking if he could stay at the church. I felt ashamed to turn him away from staying at the church. I knew what the bible says about turning a person away in need, especially a fellow believer. I had just learned that lesson from the pastor. If a person needs something from you and is a believer, we are to give without questioning. I was working to get him out of the building quickly.

I explained the situation to him: The church now had an alarm system to keep people out at night, so staying there wasn't an option. I couldn't let him stay at my house because my wife would be angry with me for letting a stranger live with us. I knew my neighbor worked for a hotel down the street just weeks before, and I could see if we could use her discount to let him stay at her hotel.

We proceeded to the hotel down the street where my neighbor had worked, only to discover that she no longer worked for the hotel chain, and the rent was too expensive for me to put him up there. I asked him if he wanted to try another place near my work. He agreed, so we traveled to the hotel near my work. The sign advertised for $49 per night. That was a price I could afford.

We talked about his mission and ministry on our way to the hotel. We discussed his preaching on street corners and how he would speak to people about the end times. Being the young Christian I was, I had to pipe up and ask, “Why are you starting in the book of Revelations?” He might be doing it wrong by starting with such a hard book to convince people to turn to God. I explained that starting at the end might scare more people than help them to repent. I told him that people still need to be shown grace and love and to start with the book of Matthew or any of the Gospels first. I explained that people might need more time to prepare for the Book of Revelations. I knew I wasn't ready to hear about the end times yet. My time had just started with God, and I knew many people who weren't ready to see God yet.

He agreed that introducing Revelation to total strangers was complex, and we discussed where he was going. He said he would continue heading East and going to the coast. As we arrived at the hotel, He asked if we could pray together before entering. He wanted to prepare his heart and for God to be in the middle of the situation to be sure the hotel had room for him. He began reciting the Lord's Prayer. "Our Father in Heaven hollowed be thy name." He prayed out loud as I pondered why he picked the Lord's prayer. A thought entered my mind, "Everyone knows the Lord's Prayer!" I began to pray with him and asked for God to be in the midst of our situation. It seemed interesting that he chose to pray that prayer, and I followed his words.

After the prayer ended with an "Amen!" We gathered his belongings and went inside to rent the room. We walked into the lobby and asked the clerk how much it was to stay the night. She said it was $59 per night unless you were a truck driver. I said it was fine and that my new friend would like to stay the night, and I would pay for it. He looked into space to see if something was off about the hotel or if he was looking for something to take him by surprise.

The front desk clerk asked for his identification and my debit card to pay the bill. She then started typing his information into the computer. She gave him back his identification card. I looked at the identification card briefly to catch his name but only caught a glimpse of the state and the color of the ID. It was from Utah or somewhere south. I then asked for the receipt and signed the paper. The information she had taken down truly caught me off guard. The man's name was "Jesus".

I about threw up my lunch, seeing that His name was Jesus on that receipt. Looking at his name, I knew I was with Jesus

Christ. All the signs were there. Every word He spoke with me about seemed to come from scripture. When I saw His name on the receipt, the scripture from Matthew 25:35-40 came into my heart and convicted me. It is the scripture where Jesus spoke with His disciples about helping others, and when we do it to the least of these people, we have done it to Him. I was filled with overwhelming joy and helped Him to his room.

After helping him with his bags and taking him to his room, I offered to take him out to eat, but he said he had everything he needed in his bag. I prayed for his ministry, hugged him excitedly, and left him to rest. When I returned to the car, I received a call from the recruiter about the job. He told me I got the job at $23 an hour instead of the original $20. I was ecstatic! And just like the first time he called, it was after something amazing happened. Again, it felt like he was watching over my shoulder, waiting for me to finish my duty as a Christian before rewarding me to move forward.

I had to return to the church and tell the secretary what happened! Then, I had to bother the pastor. I couldn't contain my excitement. I had to shout it from the rooftops and tell my wife the whole story. God had answered my prayers. I had prayed for God to reveal himself to me so I would know it was from him weeks earlier. He blew the doors off that prayer. It was for me as He had always done, but this time, I had a huge story to tell about it. Not that I wanted this to be my reward for doing good, but I had a loving father who knew me and sent that man to our church, and God knew I would be there and where my heart was. I felt so blessed that day; it was my life's turning point.

I had a new job opportunity, a new start to turn things around, and a new direction. All I could think about was how I met a man named Jesus personally, and it changed my life completely. My life seemed to have a purpose again. By talking about my past and freeing me from my sins, God invited me into a relationship with him at that very moment. I threw away my old secular music and started listening to Christian music. I got rid of several game systems that kept me up at night.

I started coming home from work and paying attention to my wife. I still kept things hidden from everyone but confessed them to God. I still struggled with pornography. I still struggled with promiscuous thoughts. The medications were keeping my focus on things I didn't want to focus on. I was still beating myself up in the shame and guilt of my past sins. And I was learning new ways of digging a bigger hole. I found places even darker on the Internet that led to buying escorts. I thought finding Jesus was going to better my life, but it put an even larger target on my back.

Chapter 7:

2008 - 2009

Cleaning House

WHEN THE UNCLEAN SPIRIT GOES OUT OF A MAN, IT PASSES THROUGH WATERLESS PLACES SEEKING REST, AND NOT FINDING ANY, IT SAYS, 'I WILL RETURN TO MY HOUSE FROM WHICH I CAME.' LUKE 11:24 NASB

I began my new position as a contract employee. I needed to demonstrate my value before they would consider hiring me full-time, so I promptly showcased my skills and the education I had acquired over the years. However, my opportunity was abruptly curtailed.

While I was at the job, I met several other Christians who found my lifestyle weird and backward compared to theirs. They hadn't been through the things I had been describing. Some were overwhelmed by my experience with how I landed the job, and others were disgusted by my past mistakes but overlooked the offense after being around me for a time. One man stuck out as a great Christian brother and saw that I was struggling to fight the demons. I looked up to him for the short period I got to know him. He read his Bible daily and noticed I also brought mine to work.

One day, I came into the Brother-in-Christ being escorted out by security. They claimed he was not performing his daily duties but only reading scripture during work hours. He was reading his Bible during breaks, and someone was offended that he was a bold Christian. But I also brought my Bible daily to work and wore it out, getting closer to God daily. I couldn't get past my behaviors, so I kept asking God to bring me out of it and kept a journal of all of my situations. As they dragged him out of the building with a bible in hand, he hugged me and told me to keep the faith and don't give up. God had me right where He wanted me.

I started attending sexual addiction meetings per the advice of my pastor to help get me away from the pornography and the self-harming acts I was undertaking. I found myself learning about places on the Internet where you could go to buy time with women for sexual favors. Initially, I didn't go there, but the thoughts kept invading my mind. The medications were helping me at work to keep my concentration, but they also made me think of all of the sinful acts my human mind desired to experience.

One morning, I woke up with a grueling headache, and my teeth were hurting immensely. My wisdom teeth were coming in hot and hurting my head. The dentist discussed having surgery to remove the six wisdom teeth I had and what the procedure would take to remove them from my mouth.

I quickly learned that sometimes, bettering your life means losing a lot. Three months into my contract, I was hired permanently for my contract position with the new company, which meant having one fewer employer and more money. I took time off for the wisdom tooth surgery. I was told I had to go off of all medications for a time while healing from the surgery. My body started to have withdrawal symptoms, and I began picking at my body and hallucinating. Not realizing I was still not fully well enough to return to work. I followed the doctor's recommendations and returned to work the following Monday.

I caught an email that I thought was directed toward my job and performed the task. To my mistake, the medications kicked in later in the day when I realized that I had made the mistake. I quickly reported it, and I was reprimanded for doing it and fired immediately from the position. I had performed maintenance outside the company's maintenance window, and they had a no-tolerance policy for such actions. I quickly grabbed my things, put myself together, and walked out the doors with security escorting me out of the building.

As I walked out, I heard the chatter of a higher-up executive commenting on my mistake and how dumb that person was to have made such a mistake by taking down a switch in such a way. The sheer mistake was bad enough, but the humiliation of catching wind of someone so high up in such a short time truly felt demeaning.

The whole situation felt God lead but also demoralizing at the same time. It felt like Satan put me in an even deeper hole of despair, given our financial situation. After only being there for four months, I had to go home and tell my wife I had lost the job. I attempted to return to the cable company, but they refused to bring me back on. I had to file for unemployment. Was I in the wrong? Did I mess up so bad that one mistake could cost me my livelihood?

Just a few weeks before this, I had made attempts to address issues about my childhood abuse with my brother. How he had abused me. How he would beat me and torture me behind closed doors or under blankets while my family was in the room. I emailed him at work, discussing intimate details about the events leading up to my behaviors. I didn't think anything of his circumstances at the time. His company could have fired him over the communications had they taken the time to look. I was enraged with grief over my lost childhood. And he was the center target. My therapist suggested I seek amends and talk with the people who hurt me, and he was number one on the list.

I came out about all of the abuse, all of the hurtful things done to make me fearful of the dark. I held nothing back, and I came out about my part in hopes of helping to set things straight.

I tried to explain the situation and issues to my sister-in-law and how I felt my brother might be abusing my niece and nephews sexually and that my brother needed to get help as well. I explained that I had already started receiving help through therapy and counseling.

Sometimes, too much venting is enough to send people packing. The whole situation back-fired on me. My family only heard what I did to my nephew when I was 12 years old. The blame fell all on me. "Why didn't you say something when you were being abused?" I could hear the voices in my mind tearing me down even further. "How could you do that to your nephew? Do you know how much therapy he is going to need because of it?" All of my pain endured as a child came raging over me in the form of my family. They swept my brother's part under the rug as if he didn't do anything, all because he denied it, and my nephew claimed that my brother never abused or beat him. I wasn't sure if it was out of fear or if it was the truth, but I wanted it to stop, no matter the cost. It put eyes on the situation, and I said my part and left it at that. Then, I released my first book.

Relationships were blowing up around me. Secrets were coming out, and the ball of fecal matter was rolling downhill, and I was the target. My world was crumbling down all around me, and nothing I could do could save me from the pain that I was about to endure. Going through the pain again is not something anyone wants to do, but often, it is in the pain that we experience healing. And I was about to create a lot more pain for myself. I started harming myself sexually.

I had switched to a new medication that left me cold and heartless. I began to have no filter. I hurt people's feelings all around me, and I was out of control. The extreme became the normal act of the day. I was out of a job but looking. I stayed home most of the time and spent money we didn't have. I no longer just thought about acting out with women online. I hired them.

I found myself hurting others constantly. My wife, my pastor, and even my friends. When I opened up the old wounds, I discovered my past was tormenting me and cutting me down bit by bit. Soon after losing my dream career at the job God had placed me in, I went downhill fast.

Being unemployed for the first time pushed me to my limits. I now had more time to figure out what not to do with my life. My mind would wonder, and I received unemployment checks because I lived in a right-to-work state. They couldn't just terminate my contract because of one mistake. I took them to unemployment court and won. The man who walked past me in the hall as I left the primacies ate his words, and the company fell apart shortly after that. I washed my hands of the situation, but I was getting further out of control.

To keep myself busy while unemployed, I found time to volunteer at the church and call on the other parishioners to assist in cleaning the church building. We had limited the youth group that year but kept working to make things grow. I decided to work at the church and clean up the building as it was in disarray from letting the janitor go to save money and take care of the church ourselves.

One Sunday, God gave me the idea of having the congregation come together to clean up the church and shine the brass and all the corners together to revive the church building to its original glory. This was another lesson that God wanted to show me: how He cared for me throughout my days. I asked the church to show up anytime during the week and help with anything they felt needed to be addressed with the building, and we would make it happen. No one showed up, but the secretary helped me out where she could when she wasn't doing the other duties. I cleaned the church by myself that week, but God showed up, too.

One day, the church was hot and muggy, and the sanctuary A/C was turned off to conserve power. I told my wife I was going to the church to clean the sanctuary and get the woodwork and pews a good shining.

As I started at one part of the sanctuary and moved toward the altar, I ran out of breath from the heat. My body was worn down from the work. I finally walked down the center aisle, fell at the altar of the cross, and passed out. When I came too, I looked up at the cross and prayed for God to send me a worker to help me finish this job.

After I had finished praying, the secretary came into the sanctuary. A man had come looking for work, food for his family, and money to turn on his electricity. She said we could help with the money and even give him food from the pantry if needed, but she noticed I needed help.

He asked what we needed to do, and I explained that we needed to go through each pew, polish up the woodwork, and clean the floors. He took a rag and got to work right away. About five minutes later, the man who came had over half of the sanctuary pews cleaned and put back together. Then, my wife and niece checked how I was doing with the work. He had the whole sanctuary polished in 15 minutes. I had never seen anyone move so fast.

We offered him lunch and a few items from the pantry and asked if he wanted a ride home, as he had to leave soon. Then he told me about his life and that he was about to be evicted from his home. I told him he shouldn't have difficulty finding work if he worked like that for an employer.

I dropped him off near the place I was reminded of years before when the pastor arrived. The same neighborhood I had been afraid to travel around was where this man came from. God had moved me to a new level of confidence, and I was looking forward to seeing this man in the future.

He offered to return the next day and help finish the job. I suggested we pick him back up to save his energy from walking. He agreed to return and give us more assistance and said he would do as good work as he had done that day. I am still determining how it happened or why it happened. If it was the medications, or if it was an act of God, but the next day, I went by his house where I dropped him off and saw him go into the building, was gone. An empty field where a house once stood was left with grass growing and no sign of anyone living nearby.

It was as if God had sent an angel to help me understand that He would always have my back in any situation. Several other miracles happened like that as we pushed through the unemployment process. We always had enough, even though I managed to mess it up with another escort or fling. $400 here, $200 there. It was draining our account as quickly as we were getting it. I struggled to take things seriously with God. And yet, I felt called to become a pastor.

Just as I had gotten my footing and was working to become a pastor, the church's Bishop asked the pastor to move on and be called elsewhere. My friends, who were the youth leaders, saw this as an opportunity to move on, but I wanted to stay and fight. I knew the vultures would return for the remains once we left the church open. And I had just received a nomination to become an ordained minister in training.

Weeks before was the annual conference, and the Bishop of the church had asked for the names of those people who were being called into ministry. I, along with another older friend, felt the call. We were asked to have a vote for those who wanted to see us continue in ministry. My friend and I were both nominated to proceed to the annual conference. He had previously been a pastor at a church in Ohio. I had been lost up to this point in my life, but I felt God calling me to go further, even with my escapades.

The process was grueling. The time it took just to be considered for becoming a pastor was very consuming of life. In my mind, I felt ready, but my heart and God knew better. God planned to teach the whole church who He wants as a pastor, not who we think should be. The evening of the meeting, when they were to vote on us to become pastors, ended in an argument between the old guard and the new church members. The voting didn't happen that night. And I was dismayed by how they were all behaving. I was more angry at the idea that I might not become a pastor.

Filled with emotions, I sat in the entryway, crying out to God. "Why did this have to happen this way, Lord?" "Have you forgotten about me?" As I cried, the pastor realized what she had done by overlooking the vote. She apologized for the mistake and assured me that God was still in control and that there would still be a vote in the future. She assured me I had what it took to become a great pastor.

Three weeks later, we had another conference to vote on whether or not my friend and I were to become pastors. The old guard and new church members were there. We listened to the District Superintendent discuss what it means to be in ministry and serve God with all our hearts. Deep down, I knew I wasn't ready to become a pastor, but part of me wanted it.

The church took a private vote on paper and placed it in a ballot box. The votes were counted 11 yes' to 7 no's for my friend. That is not surprising, given the room of people. Then came my results. 11 yes' to 7 no's. The totals for the vote were the same for the older friend as they were for me. The result took everyone by surprise. The old guard didn't want me to be in the pulpit because of my past. The new church members knew where I was and where I had come from. Now was a time of change.

Shortly after that, my pastor was called away, and we were off to a new church body and a wacky pastor who gave out shot glasses to people who were in the bar too often. It felt like family and friends from the start. We were greeted lovingly, and the pastor, while not as educated as my mentor, offered something different that I hadn't seen before. He was an evangelist at heart and loved introducing people to Christ. It was just what I had been missing.

My friends who helped me when we were leading the youth group had left just two weeks before and told us about this pastor who had awesome ideas and a unique way of reaching people. He would go into the dark places of people's lives, walk alongside them, and, with God's help, pull them out of their pain and suffering and into a new way of life.

The pastor had started a new church plant in a nearby town, gathering people's attention quickly. People were excited to be there, and it seemed like God's word was being preached. He was a licensed local pastor who had left a corporate executive job to go into ministry. He helped people see the stories about Jesus were real, as I had experienced. This made me want to follow him all the more. So we left the old church for a new beginning, hoping to find freedom from my past sins.

HERE ARE MY JOURNAL ENTRIES FROM THIS POINT ON ABOUT THE REST OF THE STORY.

God, YOU ARE AMAZING!!!!!!!

I received a call today that felt exactly like the call from my last employer, including the part of God helping me with anything and everything I need. This job pays $23.00 per hour, the same as the last job. I felt like God was saying I didn't do anything wrong there, and he wanted to bless me and restore me to my previous state. I am meeting a recruiter I called out on a whim to ask about a position. I was ready to volunteer my life even if it meant working for free, but God, you pulled through for me in my time of need.

As I received the recruiter's call, the radio came on with the songs: "Something Beautiful" and"Sing, Sing, Sing". God, you showed me today that you have something beautiful in me, and I want to sing it out to the mountains.

While I know there may be others with a worse story than mine, I am writing for those who have yet to speak out about their past lives. I am speaking out about how God gives new life to those who have hurt others. I hope my story will help others stop the abuse. This is my story, and I encourage those with similar stories to seek the help they need, just as I did. I know I will continue to do so.

I believe God has a plan and a calling for every man and woman. Today, I pray that everyone will find God as I have. If my story touches your heart, open up to God. Look to God to change your life and follow his commands. If you listen to God's word because of my story thus far, I know I have done my part in God's will for my life.

My thoughts and actions have started to change toward God's will for my life. More than ever, I can say my life has never been better. I have lost control over my will, and I love it. Each day brings new life, and I feel alive for the first time.

Over the weekend, I lost myself in bike riding and being outside with my wife. I even gave up video games to help another person. One thing that shocked me was the congregation's lack of faith. It was like my old church body, which wouldn't even open its doors to its brothers and sisters. I felt embarrassed about their holding back and stepped forward to do what no one else would.

This is my first time writing in this journal in over a month—it has been a long time. I have tried my hardest to find where God is leading me. While I can't physically see God, I know he is there and real.

This morning, I woke up alone for the first time without my wife's assistance. The only thing I can attribute it to is my newfound lack of playing video games before I fell asleep. I went to the Monday addiction meeting, and I got a lot out of it, including the idea that I was addicted to video games, so this was a bit of a first step into my recovery process.

Also, at the meeting, I discussed my recovery process. After all the talking, I finally realized I had given good advice to others but had yet to follow it myself. I mentioned to others in the meeting that one way I can communicate with God is through prayer, and another is through writing in my journal.

That advice is something I hadn't been doing for a whole month. I hadn't listened to my advice mainly because I was always lying and believing the lies I told myself. While the concept sounds strange, the idea behind it, inside my addictive mind, caused me to ignore the world around me. The truth is that I was scared of sexual predators when I realized that I was one. It was in this way of thinking I was lying to myself. I had created a deceptive and unseen life I was trying to hide from the world around me.

It is this lying process that causes an addict to think that nothing is wrong with them and that everyone else is crazy. This lying process creates a way for our morals to decay. The lies change our minds and alter our view of the perfect world we once saw as addicts. We can turn on the lights and realize the chaotic path we truthfully thwarted behind us. And where is God in all of the chaos? He is one step ahead. He waits for us all to land on our faces after tripping over our self-made lives. We are still stuck somewhere deep and more profound without him to lead us out of the muck.

Even now, I can see God laughing at my past. He told me I didn't know what I was thinking or doing at the deep end of my life. He is also glad that I made it back to shore and I was not dead again. He is pleased that I can now pay attention to his will for my life.

To sum it all up with even more creepiness, I saw an old friend whom my sponsor suggested I contact. I discovered that my friend works at the same place where I was recently hired. His number was kept in my notebook for my journal. His number was also on my laptop, where I kept my journal to write about how God's call has worked for me thus far.

I spoke with my friend, and he talked to me about his addiction to alcohol and the lure it had on his life. He showed me a great deal of compassion. Even more impressive is that the other people in my life are all looking in the same direction as I am.

The man who sits across from my cubicle was going into seminary school but fell out of touch with God's call for his life. A woman who works at the first desk in my row had a nephew in the hospital with Meningitis in his brain and pneumonia in his lungs, and the doctors thought he had swine flu to top it all off.

She came to me one day before Thanksgiving to ask for prayers for her three-year-old nephew. She asked me to put her nephew on the prayer chain at my church. Due to the chaos, I was disjointed from my old church's prayer circle. That night, the church called to ask about a prayer for another person, and I asked for prayers for that little boy.

That Thanksgiving, her nephew was out of the chemically induced coma. The doctors were done with surgery on his head. He was looking well, and he was fighting with his sister and eating Thanksgiving dinner in the hospital with his family.

Just when I thought God was done for the day, He only began to show me what His power can do over my life. I am powerless over God's will to manage others in a world I thought I created. I finally realize that no matter how much effort I put in to achieve greatness, the world I live in is merely a speck of existence when viewed from God's perspective. Nevertheless, God still loves us unconditionally with the same intensity.

Tonight, I saw God's point of view closer than I might have liked at first. After volunteering to lead the meeting, I realized that the person who was late and the night's speaker was sharing his first step in the addiction meeting. The first step is to admit we were powerless over our addictive behavior. We couldn't manage our lives or anything else because that addiction controlled our behaviors and took us away to our self-made paradise.

After hearing his first step, I fully understood a crucial part of my recovery theory through the words spoken by others. Those words were powerful and loving. They encouraged me and were engraved into my soul. Once written down, the truth is absolute. The words clarified the situation once they were written down and opened for others to see.

And so, in writing in my journal, I have made progress just by releasing the truth of my abuse and addictions and sharing in my sobriety and the progress I have made thus far. It is a tool and a way for me and for others to see how addiction of any kind works and affects not only the addict's life but the lives of others around them and the people who are hurt in the process. One thing I was praying for was the day I could indeed start writing my story. And God has shown me that today is the day to start!

Today, we learned about my wife's grandfather's passing. He had cancer for months and was without his beautiful wife for three years. He was lonely living at home and losing his memory. I think he was truly ready to go. We took a family picture with all three couples on a lake, and we had to transpose her grandpa's picture into the photograph to show that he was there with us. I was asked to superimpose him into the group and make the changes, and it turned out well, but it was a bittersweet moment upon his death. It would be another trip out of town at another funeral brought to us by the Catholic Church. I liked the church ceremonies and found them interesting. I even snuck in communion wine, being a protestant.

It felt like a cold day for the family as there seemed to be a dark separation from everyone there. The two grandparents were the glue that seemed to hold the family together, and the strength of the family was beginning to unravel around all of the children. Only God knows what could be in store.

Chapter 8:

2010 - 2011

The Jump Around

AND JESUS ANSWERED AND SAID TO THEM, "TRULY I SAY TO YOU, IF YOU HAVE FAITH AND DO NOT DOUBT, YOU WILL NOT ONLY DO WHAT WAS DONE TO THE FIG TREE BUT EVEN IF YOU SAY TO THIS MOUNTAIN, 'BE TAKEN UP AND CAST INTO THE SEA,' IT WILL HAPPEN. MATTHEW 21:21 NASB

I am still waiting for a change today, but the day is ongoing. I did get to start training again for more access at work, which, for now, means I can stay at my new bank job even longer. The past several days have been frustrating. My birthday started slow, but things improved after I visited my friend's new home out of town. I saw my friend, whom I hadn't seen since high school, and we caught up on some missing items from a previous conversation.

Slowly, my brother and sister-in-law are working towards forgiveness for my past issues. I don't believe that my brother will ever admit to his abusive behavior towards me. All I know about that situation is that I owned up to what I did those years ago, and now those issues are gone for me. Only time will tell, and I pray for God's guidance daily.

For Christmas, I gave gifts to my brother and his family. My parents said they enjoyed the game and loved the gifts very much. Although I miss them all, I believe I should stay away and pray to God so they can work through their relationship difficulties. I hope they realize that being honest with each other daily brings them one step closer to healing from their past mistakes.

As I said, the past several days have dragged on with dread, even into the new year. My patience has grown thin over many things. I wanted to be healed right now. On our way home from leaving our friend's home, our car's check engine light turned on on New Year's Day of all days. Making it home with this type of trouble might have been a problem if I didn't check it out. So, we stopped at a resting station along the highway. The sign on the exit said it was a modern rest stop. That meant one without anything around, including lights. A semi-truck was parked there along with a van, probably resting from the long trek across the country.

The only modern thing about the whole area was the skimping on the cost of building a place to serve the traveling people. I think the state should call those areas "Squatting Areas." There was no place to go but in the snow. Someone would have seen it if I had to use the restroom. Or I would have frozen something off from exposure to the negative temperatures outside. But again, I want to thank God for guiding me to the right place and time.

God pointed me to the place under the hood where the car had made a noise piercing the cold air. In all the darkness, I found the issue with the help of the light from the midnight sky and the moonlight. Talk about feeling vulnerable.

I felt like I was going to kill myself and my wife by stopping for so long in the cold night air, but not intentionally. I found the issue. It was a hissing hose. I placed my fingers on the hose and watched it crumble as I checked for where it was leaking.

As I felt it break apart, the car started to sputter and die, like our hopes of getting out of there and home that night. If there were any tools to help, it would have to be Scotch tape. I had some in the car and could tape around the pipe to keep it in place. Some people at my church said I did better than MacGyver.

I know nothing about cars and am as far from a mechanic as possible. Mindlessly, I taped the pipe in the dark and prayed it would hold together for the ride home. I used the night sky as my light in the cold, dead winter.

God guided my hand as I taped the hole up, and we watched as the check engine light went off. I managed to get the pipe back on and make it work, and it held together all the way home. I genuinely believe God got us home that night.

I just realized today at lunch that I may have forgotten to take my medications for ADD, depression, and anxiety. I have been very irritable and aware of issues being addressed at my workplace. While my addiction is sleeping, I know that it could come out at any moment. I believe it is trying to come out as my aggressiveness is increasing towards some people's suggestions at work, which may compromise my job or, at the very least, my quality scores for my performance. I feel awake today, and I almost feel like my depression has left my body. Maybe it is gone, or it is perhaps my addictive mind trying to trick me again.

I have been writing for several hours on this page, but I still need to fill most of it, unlike what I did on Monday. The weather prediction for snow is about 9 inches by the end of the day, and there will be more by tomorrow. This makes me wonder whether or not we will be having youth group tonight. I am anxious to go to see the new youth group leaders. I hated that one of them didn't get to have a party on her birthday, but I am over it for now. I wonder if her husband knew how much he hurt his wife's feelings by going to help a friend instead of celebrating his wife's birthday and being with her on that day.

I shouldn't have worried, but I didn't see how his wife's birthday was less crucial than helping his friend with a car. Then, I thought I was looking at it the wrong way. I was bashing him in my mind, and I wanted to make his wife feel better, but what if his friend was stranded?

That example is something I would do for someone I knew on my wife's birthday, too. Maybe God put that all on her husband's heart for a reason. Perhaps it was all to help his friend out in a situation. In all situations we encounter, I thank you, Lord.

And if it is just a reminder to all of us who you are, thank you again, Lord. You love me for who I am and what I was before I truly knew you.

God,

As the father of Jesus Christ, I understand that sacrifice is hard to deal with. Your plan was always to have that happen to Him so that only you could be glorified by His people. Your son represented you very well, and I will follow Him with all my life so that I can try to sacrifice my own life in return. But I want not to repay the debt but to show my love for you. Like Jesus, I am one of your children; I will dedicate my life from this day on to abstain from sinful acts as you present them to me to sacrifice those earthly things that come for my life. Amen!

It has been five days since my last journal entry—it feels like over a week. A lot has happened since then. I have spoken with my friend, whom we visited from out of town, about how she feels unwanted by her husband and the world. I spent about seven hours with my friend I grew up fighting beside in Tae Kwon Do. I also plan to do physical training with him and his dad tonight.

My wife and Dad suggested we go to the casino and spend some time there. We won money but later discovered that the bank overdrew our checking account by nearly four times our winnings. I called the bank back yesterday and faxed my statement to the claims people. I hope to get my money back from them today.

I am worried that I hurt my friend's feelings by telling her that I loved her and that she would be alright to continue to do things for herself. It is incredible to me that the same things I went through two years ago she is now experiencing, too. I mean down to the letter—depression, guilt, sadness from a loved one, or in our case, a spouse.

I felt that God put me in this position to help her since I was doing the same things myself. I pray that whatever comes of it, I am doing God's will, not mine. But I still can't get over feeling like I hurt her in some way, too. I told her I tried to be with her on my birthday in high school, and her response might have hurt me worse than if I didn't know. I am glad to see that I could have had a chance. I am blessed and happy with who God gave me.

My wife is my best friend, above all else. She loves me for who I am, and I can't accept her for anything less. I know that I treat her like crap some days. I don't mean to direct it at her, but it is directed at her attitude toward my addiction. I love my wife as much as I love breathing air, but sometimes I find breathing hard.

I know that no one else compares to my wife in my life. I only wish I could explain my addictive behaviors to her better. I sometimes think I have corrupted her mind to want things from this world. When we first met, she didn't care about material things; now, that seems all she thinks about.

I want her to seek help with her parental issues and stop trying to hide from them. Is this a problem for me, or do I need help understanding? I do know that I love her so much, but I don't know how to help her.

Today, I left my cross and my medications on the table beside my bed. Last night, I couldn't sleep, so I got up at about 2 AM, went to the kitchen, and grabbed a water bottle. My mouth was so dry most of the night. I read about roundworms, which my cats got from a stray kitten we let into the house for a day or two. I didn't get to meet with my Tae Kwon Do friend yesterday to work out, but I did make it to the Monday night addiction meeting. It helped me a lot to talk about my frustrations. While I was gone, my friend from high school called and spoke with my wife about pregnancies. I don't know if she is, but if God is willing to give us the chance to be parents, we will make it the best we can.

Each day in my role seems more promising for continuing my career. I don't want to get my hopes up, but I am getting a permanent badge soon. I am being added to the employee database as I write these pages. I hope this career is leading me toward God's will so that I can continue to share God's love for his people with others.

Lately, there have been times when I have felt like God hasn't been the center of my life. I miss his call to get up and do his work. While I know God loves me no matter what I have done, it is sometimes hard to understand where God wants me to be and why I am heading in a particular direction.

My financial situation is making me feel insecure. I know that God is looking out for me in these times. I wish I hadn't had so many hard times with money. I want to help others in need, and I know there are people out there who are in worse shape than I am, and they need more things than I do. And I want to figure out how to get my addictive behaviors out of my life forever.

I feel blinded by something, and I can't see where that next addictive episode is coming from; it makes it even harder on the finances. I need to look harder and remove these addictive obstacles from my life. I need to rely on you more, God! That is why I am writing all this down on a page: to find answers. I do it on paper instead of a computer because it is too tempting. Craigslist and Backpage are just a click away.

My prayer for today is that as I seek God's will for my life, he will help me overcome my defects of character and my desire to control my life. I want to listen to God and be truly free.

God, please guide me to set boundaries on my thoughts, words, and actions throughout the day. Teach me your will so that I can share your wisdom with others. Please work through the people you bring into my life and perform miracles. Though I am poor in wealth due to my greed, I trust that you, God, can remove that from me and guide me on the right path.

God, I pray that you will always be able to reassure my life each day I am here that I can safely rest in knowing your will over my life is one that you can genuinely say I loved you in return, but only as much as I could encompass you through your people. To point out the power of God and prayer, I just got a call at 1:40 PM from my recruiter about extending my contract until the end of 2010.

Violence begins in the mind and turns outward. At first, I think of video games as fun, exciting, and a hobby under control. As an addictive mind, I have set myself into a tailspin of messed-up behaviors that I can't seem to break. I started to work different angles of recovery only to have another habit cause more damage than the first.

God forgive me for what is on my mind right now. Forgive me for what is in my heart at this moment. Help me remember to have serenity and keep it close to your spirit here on earth so I can reach you through my faith. I believe that video games are causing me to disregard the world, and I think that those same games are causing me to ignore my friends, family, and those whom God is calling me to help find the spirit of God and continue the pattern to break free.

Sometimes, I can't stop feeling sad for others because they aren't enjoying life like I am now. That is where Satan is working in my life right now. Each day I live, he pries in my heart and shows me who I am, and I can't break away.

God,

I am weak right now. Please give me the strength and courage to resist my temptations. Make it easier for me to rely on you, not my own will but your will alone. Thank you for everything you give me. I want to love you more, but I also need to learn to love myself more and be grateful for the life you have given me. I have difficulty loving myself right now, but I know you love me so that I will try!

If we are truly honest with ourselves, how sinful are our thoughts? How wicked are we? I was trying to find a pencil that rights, something so simple, yet it took me a while to find one that writes. I had nothing in three of the five pencils I attempted to write with. I had a pencil with all the lead in the world but a lousy eraser and a pencil that would be perfect, except that someone looking over my shoulder had to have a pencil to write in her appointment book. So I gave it to her and kept the one with the lousy eraser. I kept that one because I believed God would provide me with the words and the ability not to make a mistake.

God,

Please be that cleaning eraser of my past and help wipe my slate clean of my past sins so that you can truly be magnified in all of my inequities, and in these problems, allow me to stay faithful and true to your word. Please keep me in your grasp that I might not sway from you until I return home to you. Amen!

May your love ring through my heart so that the world will hear the beating of your rhythm and not my own will.

This also reminds me that I need to slow down and allow God's word to flow through me like water and wind flowing freely throughout our days of chaos and destruction. Truly, I am never alone as long as I have God in my heart.

I am very detached from the world right now, and lately, I have become afraid of those who give me advice, specifically the group I associate with in the addiction recovery meetings.

It has been a month since I last wrote in this journal. Life without writing and communicating with God has been more difficult than I had originally thought possible. I have attempted to beat fate by returning to my old behaviors. Mainly escorts and prostitutes on Backpage.

I know I can't take back what I have done or the hurt I have caused, but I can change my mind and not return there again. I can change my mind to follow God's will and get into God's word more closely than I have. One thing I noticed is that I have been tempted several times. I didn't act on them, but I hit some bottom-line behaviors that could have caused me to act out.

By journaling these events, I hope to help others and myself. I am told there is no cure for this disease, and right now, I believe that too, but I am going to keep fighting and looking. There is a cure, and it is the truth, and I am sharing that truth with others with love.

That is the cure. Love from God cures everything, but something is still in the way. Intimacy is beautiful, but it is not like love. Many people seem to think that love and intimacy are the same thing, but I have lost almost all of the things I was intimate about. After I had lost all of the things I thought loved me, all I was left with was dust and a broken heart. God picked up the pieces and put me back together again.

God has never given me everything I wanted; I am glad he didn't. I tried to fight for it all, but Satan always wins those battles. If there were a word to describe my experiences, it would be love. God has shown me so much grace and love to abound for eternity. And I go ahead and screw it up again by slipping back into my habits and comforts of this world.

I was let go from another job, this time for being late and out of touch with reality. I don't know what I'm going to do now. God, help me face what I must do to get through today. Keep me focused on you. Please give me a sign to return to you and not return to my old ways.

Finances have gotten so difficult that we are leaving the house to move back in with my parents. It isn't something we want to do, but my addiction has caused this. I have caused this to happen. I am unsure what God's plan is for us to move back in, but I know it is God's will.

In the past few days, I have made several bad decisions. The first was spending $200 on an escort; we needed that money for bills. Being jobless and coming up with that kind of money led me to sacrifice several things:

movies, video games, and most of all, the time and trust of friends, family, and the people who love me.

While I haven't had a sober day all week until today, I am not sure I know any more about my addiction than when I started. I know that I am scared that I might be losing my dad, but even that doesn't scare me as much as the way I have been trying to lose myself in sex.

I have been trying to return to my old habits. I must temporarily stop playing video games and watching television. However, this will cut into my social time with my family and wife, mainly because that is all they want to do.

I feel triggered to act out while watching or hearing things around me or on television. What scares me worse is that I feel worse when I am alone. When I am alone, I feel ashamed and scared, and I feel like no one is watching, so I want to act out.

I am afraid to go back to work because how I lost my last two jobs due to my illness and a lack of concentration. I am still determining how I will act around people or if their attitudes will cause me to dive further back into my addictions. I am also regularly tempted to buy the latest video games. I can taste the eagerness of the voice saying I want to get it. I have got to have it.

Today, I felt so alone early on, but I managed to fight through the urge to masturbate. It hasn't become more accessible, but I haven't made it easier to stop the behavior.

Being out of work has proven both a blessing and a curse. It has been a blessing that I can take this time to heal and reflect on what has been plaguing my mind all of this time, and it is a curse because my mind continues to go back to a place where my addictive mind wanders and locks down my thoughts. It keeps me trapped in looking at pornography and escort sites.

My thoughts have become so invasive that today, I signed up for various porn-type newsletters because they portrayed my fantasies and left me wanting more. They played into the idea that I wanted to be with more than one person at a time and have another woman on the side. I am not sure why my mind won't stop, but I find it disgusting for the most part, but I am still there.

I don't know how these sites get all of the women to pose for such filth, but it is designed to focus on men who are addicted to sex. It not only keeps the focus on those who are addicted to sex but also on a large variety of people with different issues. How much detail they cater to those trying to find something untrue is scary. The idea that sex sells is nothing short of the big picture on these sites. I fear that even those who once opposed these sites are now being lured into them with lies and becoming advocates of such a problem.

The only way I have found to stop going to these sites and stay off of them is to cut off my supply, get rid of the Internet, and block myself from all the sources. This also means that I have to go to meetings, talk about the issues I am facing, and share my thoughts and problems with others who understand the pull of these sites.

Jesus was discussing this when he said we must gouge out our eyes and cut off our hands to break free from sin. He also said the truth will set you free. However, a part needs to be added to that statement. Continuing to tell the truth and not returning to the lie will set you free, but returning to it only worsens the situation.

Today, I heard a sermon that touched my heart in a way that could only have come from God. It was about baggage and the things we all carry around with us. The sermon made so much sense that it affected me in many ways. I can't let go of certain items in my life and have difficulty letting go of people.

I get to the point where I need them more than air. I feel betrayed when these people waste my time and leave me hanging on a thread. I allow them to have power over me, and with that comes the problems. These people take time away from what I can see really matters, but I still allow them to overrun my life daily.

In the past, I have turned my life over to video games, pornography, sex, and food to fill the void that was missing in my life. People would constantly criticize me for every move

I made. I feel the only way to do anything decent for myself is to isolate myself in a video game where I can be the hero who never makes a mistake and saves the lives of innocent people against the evil powers in the game.

I feel less than adequate around my friends and family. I look at the way others look at me, and I think they see the sinful, hurtful, and stain-filled person who is only capable of sinning and never, indeed, someone who can love others.

I explain to people that love has been absent for many years, and they can't grasp it. It has been so long since I truly felt love, and I don't even know how to love myself because I don't know if I have ever seen anyone share it with me other than Jesus' example.

People who say they care for me eventually leave me empty and drained. I fear trying to make friends because of this fact and the abuse I endured hatred growing up. I want to patch up the past with those I have hurt with my actions before I move on to the next person. However, this might not be realistic.

When I try to patch up the past of those people I have hurt with my actions and words, they make me feel even worse, as they have isolated me from breaking them again, and I don't blame them. I did many horrible things. I have difficulty setting boundaries and don't always notice how others act toward my words. I am learning to set boundaries, but having no boundaries before now is hard to set good ones.

There are many people I am now setting boundaries around so that I don't get hurt again, and I have now set boundaries around those who I have hurt so that I don't further open their scars. Sometimes, those people try to force their way back into my life and try to kill any hope of recovery for myself.

I must build a solid foundation in Jesus, but I need help deciding how much to share with strangers. This is probably why so many people have closed their doors on our relationship: I share too much now and don't set boundaries for what I say.

Right now, to tell what I truly feel is not knowing what love is. Feelings of love expressed by others are something I didn't know. I was afraid to trust people who said that they loved me. That was where my abuse came from. To never be abused and never held in a genuinely loving fashion for nearly 15 years of your life, and then expect that abused person to see the world the same as everyone else is just as crazy as being abused.

People who have never been abused cope far more manageable than a person who has been abused their whole lives. Abused men and women tend to have an unloved past. They tend to shy away from others, and with good reason. Expecting a different result from that person who was never held lovingly and expecting them to be controlled in their actions and forcing it to happen is just as damaging and abusive in the eyes of the abused person. Everyone needs to be listened to and loved. Correction comes later when they learn it is wrong to act a certain way, but only after they have been shown real love and kindness towards their hurts.

Yesterday afternoon, I learned that one of my friends had read my book "Bigger Than Me!" and was offended. To me, this is a good feeling. I wrote it to be offensive and make people stand up and say this isn't right and we should do something about this sort of thing. They claimed to be very close to God but couldn't see past the abuse I did to someone else. That tells me they have much growing up to do, as do I.

I am not trying to push people away from God in telling my story, but to have people look past what they have done and see the broken person, not their past actions. I am trying to show people how to share God's grace. It is not that these people don't deserve to be punished for their actions, but that there is a time for forgiveness and to help them understand why their actions were wrong. In this world, we tend to punish and then leave it at that point and never correct that person's actions. Then they go right back to doing it again.

Many people tend to have the behavior of solving the problem by locking it away and throwing away the key as the answer instead of looking into the reason behind the problem in the first place. I don't believe we are ever going to solve the problem of addiction, including sex addiction, by just sweeping it under the rug. We need to bring it out into the light and show people that it is wrong to treat people as objects. The pornography industry doesn't want you to see slaves. They want you to see people making free choices to do things and make money. If they see a desperate person trapped without a place to go and forced to do what they are doing, no one will buy their brand.

As a church body, I have experienced the same issues that have repeatedly arisen. People need to be loved no matter what their past looks like. We need to see people for who God has made them, not for what we think they are. When we doubt that people can change, we doubt ourselves and who Jesus is. I believe it is this doubt that causes people to commit suicide and turn away from the very God who created them and wants to love them. God wants to change us away from our past issues. He wants us to look ahead to what he meant for us to become.

Yesterday, I spoke out of concern that I had done something wrong. Still, in reality, after learning the true answer about why I was shunned, it was, in fact, the idea that I was still the same person I was before, and had they come to know me now instead of knowing me for my past, then I might not have had the courage to write my book or tell the truth about my past. I might have continued acting out the same way I had before. I know that I have sinned, and I continue to ask God to forgive me for those sins every day. I reflect on God's love and grace because he has shown me mercy and love.

Recently, I have been praying for God to speak to me more clearly and allow others to forgive me. Today, my prayer was answered in a sense. I asked God to talk to my friend youth pastor friend about forgiveness of my past. I recently spoke to her about something God had put on my heart and how she seemed to be judging and treating me. She was judging me based on my past life and my book. She saw how others were reacting towards my book, following the reactions of those who read it and pushing me away.

I gave a copy of my book to her husband, a pastor himself, as a token of my gratitude for helping me to get past the issues I addressed in the book. I shared my story of redemption, moving on with my life, and the gift that Jesus Christ offered me through his salvation. In doing so, the book has caused hurt feelings towards my life to the point of isolating their entire family from my presence. In doing so, it has caused my heart to grieve greatly.

After I pondered the thought of her actions, I quickly prayed for her heart to open and change with God's help. I promptly went to several brothers and sisters in Christ to point out what I felt was the issue; I drew enough courage from God's love over me to call and ask her about the reason for her isolation from my presence, and to my surprise and the words that were given to me before the call from my pastor, it was from the hard to read message from my book that concerned her about my presence.

It turned out my pastor was dead on. It was at that moment that I realized that she wasn't quite ready to deal with the issues my book addressed, as she was also abused growing up. My book had opened that wound, and she didn't want to confront me with the issue, so she isolated herself.

I had seen her verbal and physical actions toward me over the past several weeks, especially when we practiced at church with the band. I initially felt that my book clearly stated that what I did was in the past and that I was past it all, but that was not the case with her.

I believe that Satan was attempting to cripple my ties to the family I had been helping to make in the church. The book made me realize that the message was a hard one to address, and so it has been causing a lot of discord for the pastor and many others in the congregation.

I am still praying that others who judge me for my past will forgive me. While they are stuck in the past and have moved on, I pray that my book isn't keeping them there. My new pastor's friend reminded me today that God has received me, which is more than enough to fulfill my heart's desires. I need to continue to forgive those people who judge me unjustly.

I thank God for my past experiences and even more for the courage to write them down so that one of the most complex struggles many people deal with today might be illuminated by God's love. Then, the person can be free from sin and see how their past deeds don't hold them back from their future with God and Jesus.

Every day, I am renewed and revived from the slumber of my past. I am reminded of Paul's story about how Jesus showed him the way to God's love, how he was sinning by killing God's people, and how Christ turned Paul's life around for an even greater testimony to those who believed before him. They feared his disloyalty might be held in deceit towards the other disciples who were among them during his transition. Most of all, God is mighty in this respect. To use the weak to humble the strong.

This morning, I was awoken by a loud bang. Usually, I attribute this to my parent's clumsy behaviors, but it also awoke me something for my heart to do more forward-moving action in my life. More noise arose and became an annoyance to my sleeping body. The creeks of the old floor of my family's home kept me awake. I began to pray to God about the whole situation in my life. My wife and I left home to return to my parents' house. Last night, my wife and I watched the movie "Facing the Giants." As we watched, I pondered our situation and what I was doing with my life. I thought about why God had placed me here, why I was struggling with money and finances, and my church situation.

After being awakened by the pounding thuds of my parents' trampling feet, I realized that maybe I was on my way. I was an obstacle to my growth in Christ. I was blocking my way to see God's will for my life. I stopped short of God's goal and did not see it through.

Today, my grandmother passed away in her sleep on her birthday of all days. She was 90 years old. I didn't know if she was a Christian, but I knew she showed me love more than anyone else. She had caught me in my abusive behaviors and took me aside to tell me it was wrong for me to do such things when I was a child. I didn't listen to her advice much back then, but I wish I had done so now.

She gave her life to God's care a long time ago, but she grew up in the World War II era and didn't share much about their faith but lived it out daily. A bible under her bed was proof that she was in God's word daily, and it was something that was given to me after she had passed that reminded me that we never know who is under God's protection.

My heart keeps tugging at me to speak with my aunt about my Grandmother's house. I have been feeling like God was calling me to the task of not only bringing things to light on the whole issue of what to do about my uncle now that my Grandmother has passed on but also the fact that no one else can take care of my uncle, and we are without a home right now, too. It seemed like the perfect storm.

My aunt has claimed that I shouldn't be with my uncle due to my past abusive behaviors, but I say that he was more abusive than I ever was; ultimately, I see her mindset as greed at this point. God has a plan for my wife and me to be where we are right now, and I believe God wants us to move in with my uncle and help take care of him, but my aunt doesn't see it that way.

This might be a hard lesson for anyone who doesn't believe in God, but I know God has a plan for all of this. Although I wonder what the outcome will be, it doesn't put doubt in my heart that God is looking out for me today.

Right now, I am praying on paper to help reflect God's will for my life and how powerful God is by talking with my aunt about the whole situation. I have been pushed into how God's will and plan for my life will carry a more significant light to people in today's society. My message is that God does exist and that he wants a relationship with everyone in the world. I am writing this as a statement that God is in my heart and not from my own will, but the fact that God has shown me how to love others unconditionally and that God is alive and real.

There are days when I wish I hadn't written my first book, but then I realize that I am no longer the same person I was back then. I don't want to return to the old ways I used to think. While people are questioning me about my past and the motives for writing it, I think to myself that the whole idea was to show people the damage caused by childhood sexual abuse and the problems with keeping it hidden. It is not who I am now.

My past is just that, my past. Satan keeps trying to remind me of it and pull me back there through the people who are still in my life. While I know how the truth hurts through what I did, I pray that people will understand that I am not the same person back then as I am today. God and His love for me make me who I am today. My past no longer has a hold on me.

Those who can't forgive me will have their say, but they will be wrong in the eyes of the Lord. I pray for God to show them forgiveness and to remove anger towards me from their heart. I believe that God has put me in this position because he knows I am strong enough to fight this battle, and I think that He will see that I am prepared to fight against the injustices that are shown to this world today, such as sex and love addiction.

One day, my book will be noticed as something more significant than I had planned. It is getting noticed as plain filth, garbage from my past, and nothing else. The hope is that my story will take notice of this sex addiction problem the world is facing, and people will see the destroyed lives as something more significant. I believe that Jesus did rebuild the church and that he did it through people like myself. I think he took all of my sins to the cross and showed me that I am reborn, and all of my scars are evidence against those who hurt me as one of God's children. God, please help us all.

Yesterday was truly a blessed day for me. I felt like God was so close to me; it was a different experience. First, my thoughts and prayers were right on target. I listened for God to speak, and he told me a prayer would be answered when I got home. After thinking about a particular situation in which an old neighbor friend had become pregnant by a married man with four children and how he went back to his wife, I posted a prayer for her to be able to see God working in her life. God spoke to her to change her outlook and for her family to see God.

It all started five days ago when her mother appeared at my parent's house. I wasn't aware of her daughter being pregnant at the time, but someone had stolen this woman's computer out of the back of her car the day before. She went to the Big Box Store and purchased a new PC. They would charge her $100.00 to help her set it up. God put it in her heart to find me because what happened next was no longer a coincidence.

My wife and I decided to help this girl's mother with her computer. On our way to the place we had never been to, we were blocked by a road construction detour. Upon taking that detour, we stopped at an intersection, and the woman's daughter was passing us. My wife pointed out that it was her and told us to follow her. She led us right to her mother's new home.

As we approached the house, it still felt like a coincidence that she had come past us at that very moment. We exited the car, greeted the daughter and our old neighbor friend, and entered the house. While talking with the daughter and her mother, they mentioned a Christian movie about marriage, how much they enjoyed it, and how it affected their relationship with God. They told me how they would continually show it to their friends and family because of the message it sent to them. The message helped the daughter with her issues of finding out who she was in God's eyes.

My wife and I suggested two more movies from the same production company for them to watch. At this point, though, we were still unaware of the girl's pregnancy. She didn't know what to do with her new child. Excited about the first movie, she wanted to leave and look for the other two recommended movies. But only after she mentioned that she wanted to come and worship with us on Sunday.

After she left, her mother quickly told us about her daughter's situation. Her daughter was pregnant with someone's baby who didn't want anything to do with the child or her daughter. We both sat quietly and listened as her anger enraged further. While this was all happening, I realized the movie I had mentioned was about teenage pregnancy and about the people who leave relationships because they don't want to take care of the child.

I couldn't believe how much God had just worked in that moment until I heard her mother say that her daughter should have an abortion or give it up for adoption. First, she stated that this child would change her daughter's life forever. How appropriate and proper that statement was for her daughter. I pray that this child will help change how they see and live their lives without knowing God before this day. Changes are still to come for both of them. I hope this child will be a blessing and lead their hearts to God and God's grace over their lives.

The next area I saw God working was a call from a law office claiming that I owed them money, only to find out later that it was the wrong number. Then, I saw God during my evening fellowship when a new member came and was paired off with my group to talk at my addiction recovery meeting. He mentioned how he served in the military and sought a church home.

I gave him an invitation card only to find out that he had already received an invitation card from his mother in a care package that the church put together for him while he was overseas in Iraq. I helped put those packages together a time or two. It was truly unique to see how God works.

After the meeting, I discussed church with the young man more. We noticed a coat hanging on a chair. I didn't know whose jacket it was, so I took it to our group leader. Then, the jacket owner came around the corner, and I handed the coat to him. He mentioned that I had some great advice to share that night. He then explained further about a problem he was having at work and how my advice of meeting this other driver helped him out.

Another weird thing just happened as I finished the previous page to give the exact date and time I wrote the words down to indicate it was God working instead of things being coincidence alone. I looked for a clock to show me the time in the room. Yesterday, my wife brought the clock to the room. It was the only clock in the room. As I wrote these words, the clock was directly next to me as I wrote in my journal. God is fantastic, and it is impressive to see the clock where it is on the stand next to me. The words "I Am" just don't say enough about God to me! That is because He is truly fantastic, and I am proof of the love he shows the world! The alarm sounded at 6:30 AM on 11-11-2010.

In performing some research on sex addiction, I have come to a vast roadblock concerning what information is legitimate. The original idea I had been looking for was information on the percentage of sexual addicts who were abused as children. I then discovered nearly all that was studied were people who were homosexuals and not just addicts of sex.

I found sites that reported a considerable number of gay men and gay women were sexually abused as children. Still, none of the researchers recorded any actual results to calculate the percentage of people who were sexually addicted after being abused.

One study of sexually abused children indicated sexually confused children were the results of the study of those who hadn't reported their assaults as children. The results confirmed that about 2 out of 3 children who didn't report the abuse also had related symptoms of PTSD, much like that of war veterans.

Another study indicated whether or not homosexuality was genetic was only showing 27% of the survey to be approximate and that areas of upbringing had more to do with sexual preferences than the genetic findings could conclude.

Another finding of same-sex relationships, especially in lesbian couples, found that sexual abuse was less than 1%. And 0 findings on lesbians who raised children. All this concluded that sexual preference does not indicate any environmental sexual change from so-called straight families vs. gay families.

While all of these findings are good, they do not in any way conclude anything about why sex addiction starts.

My wife and I decided it was time to leave our home. The foreclosure proceedings were almost too much to bear. We had lost a lot of things due to my sexual exploits, and bankruptcy seemed to be the only option. Our new church family offered a solution and gave us a scholarship to work on our financial situation, but we were so far in debt that nothing seemed to help bring us out. So, we filed for bankruptcy and moved back into my family home. Little did I know how hard it would be on our marriage or my sanity, but God knew what He was doing.

Chapter 9:

2011 - 2012

Death Remembrance and New Life

BUT HE SAID TO HIM, "ALLOW THE DEAD TO BURY THEIR OWN DEAD; BUT AS FOR YOU, GO AND PROCLAIM EVERYWHERE THE KINGDOM OF GOD." LUKE 9:60 NASB

As creepy as it sounds, this is the first journal entry of the new year—2011 A.D. It has been exactly two months since I last wrote in my journal. The friend I played games with is back in town and living with her best friend, my big childhood friend's sister. I received even harder news: a creepy sex addict I broke ties with long ago has asked to befriend me again on Facebook. I haven't accepted it yet, but I am asking God to bring me the patience I was shown and the love that I still have been shown ever since I began my recovery back in 2005.

This recovery process has been a vicious cycle of fighting my doubts and the despair in my mind. To no avail, I have been losing ground the longer I have been here at my parent's place. As blessed as I should feel to have a place to call home, there seems to be a demonic aura around this place of safety. It seems to be attacking us at various times. The demons seem to have total control over my parents. They aren't the same people they used to be since I first moved out and back in. They have isolated themselves to the point of depression, and they have embraced its presence with great willing hearts to give the demon some form of attention.

I pray that my family here will learn God's will for their lives and that it won't be too late to change their hearts toward God. I pray that God will use me as an instrument of his will to bring my family to love and respect God. I pray that those willing to listen will embrace the word of God with me and seek to make positive changes in their lives.

My thoughts have been getting worse at wanting to act out. I have come very close to ruining my sobriety. If I am truthful, I am even violating my bottom-line behaviors and not setting myself up to succeed but to fail. Today is the first day I take my step into proper recovery.

Yesterday, I took a huge step and spoke with my gaming friend. I found out she didn't feel I had apologized for hurting her. I immediately responded from my heart and apologized for what I had done. I repented to her and asked for her forgiveness. In my heart, I knew something was wrong. It took my new observation of her actions and feelings towards me to get it out of her, but I felt like God intervened, took the reigns, and gave me the words to say.

I have been dealing with my addiction in the wrong way. It has come to a point now that I don't have to act on the temptations of porn or women, and I still feel the urges. The idea of acting on those urges has genuinely started to leave my mind. What I have found about my problems is that in a given amount of rejection and finding repentance, I am giving up my old self to others without acting out towards the idea and sexual stamina before my eyes. In a way, it is terrible because my desire to look is still there, and the desire to want others is still there, but enjoying the sex isn't there anymore.

Winter Jam Spectacular for this year was awesome. I convinced my dad to go with us and share in the fun. I saw something miraculous happen tonight. My dad had fun and saw the church I hadn't seen for a while. He was brought down to the main floor via elevator and was asked to join the front of the stage to get a better view. It was like being a celebrity. We passed all the guards and were parked right up front next to the stage, where we got the best view ever.

He jammed out with bands like Newsboys, Sidewalk Prophets, Fire Flight, Tenth Avenue North, and New Song, all of which started to change him. He even went to a prayer room and asked God into his heart last night. It was something I had never seen from him before. Something has changed in him. Jesus came in and made His house in my father's heart tonight.

Even now, I feel a battle being waged against my soul. Temptation has settled in my heart, and I have lost the power to choose. The options are whether I have sex outside of my marriage or stay committed to God and my wife.

Today, I decided to invite Jesus Christ into my heart and allow the Holy Spirit to transform me from the inside out. Just like Jesus breathed the Holy Spirit into his disciples, I asked God to breathe the Holy Spirit into my being as well. As a result, I am now a new person, reborn to a new life dedicated to fulfilling God's will for me.

A New Beginning?

During a phone interview for my first book, "Bigger Than Me: An Untold Story of Sex and Love Addiction," I was told that no matter what I said or did, I could never be forgiven by others. The interviewers were suggesting that only God could forgive me and that no human being could or should forgive me for what I had done in my past.

I have done some very evil and deceitful things up to this point. In the Bible, Jesus talks about a person's rebirth. He calls it

"Being born again." This idea Jesus shared washed the slate clean and would bring new life to the person who has sinned. It is a cleansing—a Holy Baptism through the Holy Spirit that burns away the chains and ropes that bind a person to their past.

During that radio interview, I realized I was not born again yet, at least not through the Holy Spirit. I had been searching for that transfiguration and changes of a new life to appear. It needed to be a new life, living with the Holy Spirit inflamed in my heart and burning with God's passion and power. This flame and Holy Light would guide me away from my past trespasses and sins. It would lead me back to God's grace, love, compassion, and forgiveness.

I envisioned a Holy Light coming over my body, burning away all my scars and imperfections. The idea that only God could forgive me seemed beyond belief. What I mean by that is that God created us all to be like him and to forgive others. God's Holy Spirit lives in each of us. This Spirit shows us that we must forgive those who don't deserve it. The quicker we get to that forgiveness, the less we will hurt in our hearts. I am reminded that God has humbled himself to the point of being a servant who washes our feet and not just our feet but our whole bodies. He makes us new creations.

God has allowed us to receive the Holy Spirit as a gift. This should not be taken lightly or forced out of anyone's hands. This gift has a heavy price associated with it. God came down in the image of man and took sin's punishment for us through his son, Jesus Christ. He allowed us to repent, turn away from our past, and have a relationship with Him. How much should a person be able to forgive another person? God answered that by coming down before us and taking the full burden of sin upon his only Son, who died on cavalry and was born again through God's word.

This morning, while bathing, I felt the Holy Spirit move over my body. I could sense its presence and feel the warmth of a love I had never felt. I then understood why God would leave us with such a gift. The Holy Spirit flowed all around me, and it was a fantastic feeling that could only be described as the Holy Spirit. I instantly thought of kissing my wife.

The spirit said it was all right, and I no longer needed to be afraid. It told me that I needed to know that God had a plan for my life, to let go, and to allow the Holy Spirit to guide me throughout the rest of my life. Then, it said that God would provide whatever I needed.

One day, I visited my doctor. I wasn't feeling much better after seeing him, but I knew what needed to happen. I needed to learn how to love appropriately. He said that since my parents didn't show affection and love with vulnerability and honesty, he could understand how I could not understand how to love the right way.

This both made me feel normal and like I was finally getting somewhere in my recovery for the first time in a long series of counseling sessions. The idea that I don't know how to separate love and affection from sex has bothered me for years. It was always in the back of my mind that all women were constantly being treated like trash, and it was up to me to show them love in my way of showing it.

I thought that showing a woman sex was better than the way they were being shown love because I saw sex as a device of healing rather than harm. In my mind, I knew that I was the best at making people happy through sex. It made me glad to see other people happy after sex, and I felt good about it as well.

I didn't want life to be this way, but my brother and cousins were the ones who showed me what I thought love was, both physically and mentally. Everyone else looked at me like I was broken or no good to the world. In my mind, sex was what love was. Sex is what people do to show they love you, right? My mind was finally starting to break free of this whole idea of love from my past.

Telling the truth allowed me to break free. I had to tell the truth lovingly so I wouldn't hurt others. Telling the truth about our past removes the hurts from our minds and allows us to move on.

When I was a child trying to understand love, marriage, and how to keep a girl loving me, I used to think that if I did something amazing, like making a basketball shot, the girl I was with at the time would marry me.

I must admit that as a child, my understanding of love was quite limited. I struggled to love my family and wife healthily and often associated love with sex. Looking back, I realize that my perception of love was flawed, and I need to be willing to learn and grow in this area.

I didn't want to love my father, mother, or brother that way. I thought love only had to do with sex. My brother loved me this way. Love was never used in a good and healthy way within the walls of my family home. It is no wonder to me now that I couldn't get a lot of women to like me in my youth. That might be why all the boys wanted to beat me on the playground. I couldn't begin to know how uncomfortable I was making people feel.

As my way of showing remorse, affection, love, and general hospitality, I would bring women home and touch them inappropriately. All the while, I was making it seem accidental. In most cases, I became good at reading people's faces. I became a master manipulator of people's emotions through sex. I had it in my mind that sex was the cure-all for every girl's sadness and rudeness.

My addiction had been getting more prevalent at times while living at my parent's place after losing our home to foreclosure and bankruptcy. It all seemed like it was a fresh start at first. I feel it is a new time and place, but I am still haunted by the surroundings and the environment I am in once again. I have slept around and looked for ways to act out sexually.

I received money from taxes that were overpaid, and I used forty dollars of it to have some random woman give me oral sex at a motel six and risk getting arrested once again. I want to stop my actions during this time, but it has been hard for me up to this point to find any sobriety to date. I have finally told myself I am done acting out my sexual fantasies, and I am going to do this for myself. One other area I am having trouble with is the cell phone. I have been talking sexually with people I have met online.

I knew it needed to stop, but my mind found the attraction flattering, and I seemed to crave it even more now than I did before. Then there's a girl I had been attempting to mentor that I don't have any sexual feelings for. Some lustful thoughts wanted to pop into my head, but I managed to keep them out for now.

She was just like I was when I was in high school. I let her borrow a copy of my book, "Bigger Than Me!" I am unsure if she read it, but I hoped she would be motivated to read it and not make the same mistakes I made. And I was worried she was losing sight of what mattered in life.

I had been feeling increasingly isolated and hopeless lately. My old high school friends have hurt me again, and it has been tough to deal with. I recently found out that because of my story being written, some of these friends have turned against me. It was hard to move on because people seemed unwilling to forgive me for what I had done in the past. Even my best friend's girlfriend had expressed discomfort around me because something she felt about my character was off.

That feeling was not solely based on intuition. Instead, it originated from external sources who had heard about my actions. My behavior did not give her the initial impression of who I was; instead, it was the input from our mutual friends, who had a different perception of me.

I felt terrible about expressing my feelings and wanted to keep them bottled up much longer. But the seal was broken, and the bottle was emptied on the floor for all to see. I aimed it toward them and told them how I felt, but I felt worse because they were not truthful about what was in their hearts.

I was feeling quite troubled as my friend had recently made new acquaintances who seemed to hold a grudge against me for things I had done in the past. I was surprised they knew about my past behavior as I had never discussed it with them. Despite being happy for a sex-addicted friend's progress, I was not being truthful to others. The last sentence was meant to be sarcastic. I hoped that God would help them see how much I had changed, and I prayed that it wasn't selfish of me to ask for that. Amen!

Father God!

Please hear my prayer. I want to know you more each day, but I fall short of your will for my life every day. My prayer is for you to come into my heart and change me from the inside out, and if it is through my experiences and testimony that you want me to share, keep my life, my heart, and my spirit safe if it is all in your will.

I want to ask you what you want for my life here, but I know it's not about me but you, God! I know your pain and torment match and even exceed my own by far, but the comfort you give is what I truly am seeking to find. I have yet to have seen it, in my shame. So please, if it is in your will for me, remove this shame and replace it with what you want of me. Help me focus on the truth in your word. Use me to glorify you further so that everyone you bring to my life from here on the earth will see your grace, forgiveness, and love for them through my life. At the very most, I pray for your will to be done in all of what I do in my life.

Your faithful servant in Christ,
Ryan Capital

Today, I found out that current efforts for a sexual addiction recovery presentation haven't taken off. Efforts have failed thus far, and a more direct approach seems needed to help fight this problem. Possibly talking with various strip clubs and escort agencies to see if they might be willing to help support an effort to keep their men and women safe?

Today, I ran from an addiction meeting after being told that my dad was unresponsive at the V.A. Hospital. He had been awake several hours earlier, recovering from a virus that hit him pretty hard. Later in the evening, he was found unresponsive by the nursing team. He was ready to go home and had all his monitoring equipment off him. Then, he lay down because he felt tired and never woke up.

His heart gave out on him due to plaque built up around his heart from complications due to obesity and hypertension. Diabetes didn't kill him; pancreatitis didn't take him away. Only God could have done such a thing. God stopped my dad's heart at just the right time.

I saw the changes God made in my father before he passed away. In the short time since January, he had helped so many people. He helped a homeless kid buy a pair of glasses, helped a military veteran with cancer want to live instead of starving to death, and helped a young lady escape prostitution. I also know he is forgiven of his past transgressions because he accepted Jesus Christ as his Lord and Savior. Amen!

The man I mentored and brought to Christ earlier this year would now meet God first-hand. He now appeared lifeless on a cold metal table in a veteran's hospital. The diagnosis was a hardened heart.

I became resentful at God for taking my father so quickly after he had found Him. How could God not use my Father to bring others to Christ? He reached who he needed to reach, and that was it. Jesus prepares a room and comes like a thief at night to take our lives back to His Father.

I felt lost and alone, and my addiction was getting the best of me. I had been introduced to some new church members but didn't want to hear more about recovery. I wanted chaos instead of healing at this point.

I had seen my father help a young man buy a pair of glasses after He found Christ again. He had a new breath of life in his steps, and to see that taken away really brought me to a new low. It's been a month since my dad passed. It feels as though nothing has changed. My sex addiction has skyrocketed out of control. I keep having thoughts of a threesome. For some reason, I try to help people, but it seems to get me into worse trouble than before.

I have been struggling with a certain experience that keeps bothering me and affecting my work. I think the only solution is to forget about it altogether. However, I am not sure why I wanted to have that experience in the first place. It has been affecting me to the point that I am considering creating a group to help adult male victims of childhood sexual abuse. I have been searching for such groups but haven't found any yet. Therefore, I have set a goal to create one.

After my father's death, my wife and I managed to move out of my family's basement. I was still struggling with pornography addiction and addiction to escorts. I felt as though going back to the place of abuse was hurting my recovery. I met a great number of escorts and helped a few escape that life, but how was I going to get out of the situation and back to a life free from the sinful acts of my past?

We finished filing for bankruptcy and went through a Financial Peace University program. My student loans were due, and we needed to find a way to pay them and get back on track with our finances. However, I was still unsure where God was leading me and my wife. So, we moved closer to the church and far away from the family home in hopes of starting over.

My brother moved around every 2 years and was running from me after I came out about the abuse. He tried hiding his family from the presence of my wrath. I didn't want to hurt anyone, but he tried to escape everything he thought he knew. It was almost as if God showed me every move he would make before he made it. I shared it with my mother, and she was taken off guard by all of my visions, wondering how I could have known what was happening without being involved in my brother's life.

That year, we took the Financial Peace University course for the second time. We tried to learn the course in 2009, but my wife and I were not ready to hear the lessons. This time, it started to sink in. "Save money for emergencies and don't spend what you don't have!" became our mantra for the next few years. The course brought us closer together, but it wasn't for a lack of trying on my part to bring down the house again.

I was still hurting from the loss of my father. I was sure he was in God's presence, but I wasn't sure I could ever get there, given that I wasn't stopping my exploits. Then, a new couple came to the church. It was an older couple who had dealt with similar issues we were facing—things such as sexual addictions of various kinds. At first, I attributed his recovery to his age, but he assured me it was because of God and showed me a program that helped him.

I didn't want to believe him at first. The doctors said that I would need more treatments and I could get better, but he was selling me something else. He claimed that with my book being out in the open and that my story was there to tell the world, I was still missing something, and he was right. I wasn't being truthful to some degree, but he also pointed out that something had a hold of me. That something was keeping me from moving away from sin. He said there was a program online to help me get away from psychiatric medications and that this was what may have been keeping me trapped in my sin.

I enlisted into the Cross Centered Mind program at https://www.settingcaptivesfree.com/ and quickly realized what the program was about. Then Satan came in and tried to crash the party in my mind. "I can't get off of these medications!" The doctors stated that no one ever gets off them once they are on them. The idea was that this was the cure for Adult Attention Deficit Disorder, and there was no other way. And my addiction was a result of ADD, not the medications. So, I sat on the idea for a while.

Chapter 10:

2012 - 2013

Bewitching Hours of Healing

"I CRIED TO YOU; SAVE ME, AND I SHALL KEEP YOUR TESTIMONIES. I RISE BEFORE DAWN AND CRY FOR HELP; I WAIT FOR YOUR WORDS. MY EYES ANTICIPATE THE NIGHT WATCHES THAT I MAY MEDITATE ON YOUR WORD." PSALMS 119:146-148 NASB

Today, I worked late again. I'm still struggling to straighten out my life. My therapist suggests that I work on how to forgive myself and my brother.

In addition to all the problems I have been dealing with lately, I am facing new issues that are making my situation even worse. I wish to get rid of all my troubles, but unfortunately, I keep getting dragged back into them repeatedly, like a wrestling match with God. If people only knew how much their actions affected me and triggered me to do foolish things, they would be more careful and avoid doing them.

They would continue to do them without any hesitation. Although I miss writing in my journal, I intend to do it more frequently and complete my second book. This year, I hope to overcome my addiction with the help of God and his guidance in my life.

I seemed to have misplaced my faith in a dream. I went to my addiction recovery meeting. I had a meeting tonight, and I recalled a weird but vivid dream right before I awoke to my red-haired friend needing help getting out of jail.

It seems her gambling addiction has somehow trumped my addiction to sex. Not that it should matter either way. My dream, however, had some bothersome effects on my spiritual side. It made me feel down and empty inside.

I am struggling with the loss of my father and the fear of being alone. I am constantly afraid that something tragic will happen to my mother and wife, leaving me alone in a world that sometimes sees me as an enemy because of my spiritual beliefs.

I cannot continue if I lose them. This fear is causing me to act out and struggle to keep my composure. Today, I realized I tend to overcommit myself without proper planning, often leading to negative consequences.

I am looking forward to hearing from the mentoring pastor for spiritual guidance. It seems that the pastor at the church is more focused on saving his congregation than on building God's kingdom.

There are a lot of things going through my head today. The first thing is, "What am I supposed to do, God?" Second, I want to act out and get into more trouble. Another thing that has been terrifying me is what to do about the play I am supposed to be in on Friday and Saturday.

I haven't practiced. I haven't taken much time to work hard at anything, and I don't want to disappoint my good female friend from high school or her family. It is a massive night for sexual abuse awareness, and I would feel even more ashamed and nervous about the whole deal if I failed her, too. Plus, I have a second interview with an insurance company on Friday. That is the same day as the play my friend is putting on. I know I have over-extended myself, but this is topping my anxiety charts.

I don't feel like working for anyone else anymore, but I know I have to for a while. I need a plan to break out of my shell and start my own business. One that deals with sex addiction and helping others find the right help that they need to move on with their lives. I know I am young, but I need to deal with this before someone else draws up the courage to do it and beats me to the finish line. All I know now is that God has to be at the center of the model I am building.

Today, we found out that my stepmother-in-law was found catatonic in her sleep. Completely unresponsive and not able to move. She was alive but had infection throughout her body, possibly from staff infection from the motorcycle accident in 2007. My wife's father lost his leg that year in the accident, and both of her and his wife broke a lot of bones.

Last night, we came over to their house for dinner, but we only saw her acting out of sorts. Her face seemed off and out of touch and irritable. I thought in my mind that she looked like she was going to die the next day, but I didn't say anything. She looked at me with eyes that seemed empty of a soul for a moment. I had seen that look before when I saw a dead body in the morgue of the medical examiner's office.

My father-in-law came home to the nearly lifeless body of his wife lying in bed where she had been before he went to work. He thought she had just been heavily asleep as he left for work. He came home for lunch to find her still in the same position as before he had left and tried to wake her from the sleep to realize she was not in a good place.

The ambulance rushed her to the hospital and placed her on machines in hopes of saving her body, but the staff infection had spread to her brain along with meningitis from a trip to Mexico. The combination took out a beautiful woman today. She was the last one we could see passing in the family, but the first to go. We were all surprised to see her lying there, lifeless and void of any action. I thought to myself, where are you, God? It was a wake-up call, for sure.

I have been feeling very lonely all week long. I am looking for answers to what I want to do next. I gave away money in hopes of helping a prostitute have a second chance, but in the process, I left my wife without cash in Las Vegas. I feel trapped and alone, but I know it's not true. I keep trying to ruin our relationship, and I don't want to. I keep hearing about other people's lives of sexual intimacy and wonder why I can't have that. If I did, would I be happier?

Something keeps telling me I will, but that isn't what others say to my face. I think they are lying to me to cover up some big secret so that I won't experience it, but something tells me I need to feel whole first. I have been praying for God to give me the answer, but I also want to know what answer I want.

Should I keep working or return to recovery? I can't decide. I know I need money, but I must figure out how much. I feel irresponsible and worthless. I keep hearing the right answers while trying to find the wrong ones. Which way do I need to go?

Might As Well Face it!

It has been hard for me to work and stay abstinent. I went to work this morning after a weekend of acting out behaviors. I ran around with my red-headed friend to casinos all over the state. Now, I realize my ideas are clouding my judgment and causing me to stop thinking about the consequences of my actions. I had to man up and tell the truth about what I had been doing.

My job was interfering with my recovery from sexual addiction. I had to go in and explain to my manager that I needed to be in recovery more than I needed money. I was missing meetings every time I went to work. I asked if there was any way for me to be scheduled around the meetings at least once a week. The ball is in their court, and I can now wait patiently for their answer.

Another issue I have been dealing with is the area of what to do about starting a public speaking venue where I can make a living while speaking about sexual addiction and pornography addiction issues. One thing that God did provide for me over the weekend was some answers to whether or not I should be doing it, and it was a definite "YES" for me to go ahead and start the work.

My next step needs to be where, who, and ultimately, how I will get it started. I need to figure out who wants to know and who needs to know, as well as who should know about this problem. God, please give me the answers I need to answer these questions! Help me discover what it is you want me to do next.

I just woke up from a long day of men worshiping Christ. It was amazing to see God's work and the body of Christ working so rapidly and to have it all in tune with grace and mercy. I saw flocks of Christian men drive down to the forefront of the stage to recommit their lives to Christ and be called out. It just felt like God was there, moving through us all.

You could feel God's love flowing, and worship echoed from each man's voice, singing as one body. The sound rang out through the stadium, and to hear it all go silent in unison with the songs we sang, it felt like God's voice was being heard, not the voice of men.

As for my recovery, I found out that my friend, who was selling herself on the street, is now safe and home with her mother in Illinois. She is back home and recovering very quickly, away from the people who were abusing her. My prayer for her is that she remains truthful in her words and actions and stays safe and on the road back to a better life for herself.

As for my recovery, I received good news about my treatment from my therapist. She decided to help treat my symptoms with EMDR after about a year of working with her. I pray that it will help me get over my past abuse and other issues. I hope that it will allow me to have constant sobriety for the first time.

I am at the Promise Keepers event and spoke with someone in charge of some event structure. He would like to talk with me more about my book and the possible promotion of the recovery process I want to talk to men about. God is good all the time!

I don't know what to say or do for myself today. I last ate breakfast, and it was 7 PM. My wife says she is bringing home hamburgers, but I know I don't want to cook. I hope they are from somewhere that has already cooked them; otherwise, I will go to bed hungry.

Right now, I can't stop thinking of acting out. I think it's because my mother hasn't been taking her medications for her depression, making bad decisions, and in all of her actions, I am worried about her. The other reason I feel like acting out is the nearing date of moving to our new apartment. It would be moving out of my mother's house for the first time since we lost our home, and I both dread and want to move to be independent. I don't want to leave my mom alone after just a few short months of my dad's death and with her depression.

On the one hand, I don't like being here at our family home because it reminds me of the past abuse and the memories of my brother, but in another way, I like having the safety of my family home still being here. I like not worrying about having nowhere to go if we have a similar predicament: if my mom chooses to sell her home, move to Arizona, and be with my brother and his family.

I desperately want to stay because it is home here, and on the other hand, I want to leave to be free from the abusive thoughts that haunt me and my self-mutilating tenancies.

The idea of hurting myself through sex constantly plagues me here, and the ones around me are affected by it. I have asked God for help in many ways, and I believe he will continue to come through for me every time. And I had many good things happen to me at work today.

The world didn't even end on December 21, but it did lose my wife's mom on the 17th. I haven't written in my journal for a while now. That was primarily due to my lack of confidence in myself and what I wanted to say.

There were several children killed a few days before this, and a young man who caused the problem took his own life as well. People talk about the children and wonder why it happened, and all I can think about is why it didn't happen sooner than this. I could relate more to the boy who killed all of those kids than the victims. I say this because I could have been there myself had it not been for some grace shown to me early on. I feel horrible about what happened to those children and their families. I feel awful about what I just did. I received a call from my homeless friend. He asked to attend church this morning, but I couldn't get him because I had choir practice at 8:20 AM, and my wife doesn't like to drive in the snow.

Going over my journals, even I couldn't believe today how much my actions could have cost me so much more. How would I get out of all of my behaviors? How could I be healed from such terrible actions? Why was I still not being healed from my addictive mindset? Was God really in my life, or was I lying to myself?

I was convinced that I had made a mistake in writing my book and kept it hidden, and I didn't want to promote it any further. My sin felt so terrible, and it was terrible, so much so that I felt depressed beyond anything else, and I wanted to take my own life to hopefully heal the world of my blight. I wasn't going to stop by my power, but with God's help, all things are possible.

Chapter 11:

2013 - 2014

Running from Hell

"NO TEMPTATION HAS OVERTAKEN YOU BUT SUCH AS IS COMMON TO MAN; AND GOD IS FAITHFUL, WHO WILL NOT ALLOW YOU TO BE TEMPTED BEYOND WHAT YOU ARE ABLE, BUT WITH THE TEMPTATION WILL PROVIDE THE WAY OF ESCAPE ALSO, SO THAT YOU WILL BE ABLE TO ENDURE IT."
1 CORINTHIANS 10:13 NASB

3 AM

I am tired and want to sleep, but I know you won't stop speaking to me because you love me. You want me to succeed and give you all of the glory. Incredibly, you can speak to me in so many ways. I only get the messages once it's the right time to receive them. I hope I am being as loyal as you want me to be, Lord.

I dream about you all of the time. I try to think of what you want me to do next, but this world is so damaged and torn from you that I sometimes question anything about saving it. But then I stop and think about what you did for me on the cross, and I know if there was another way to you, why would you have done what you did to your only son on that ugly cross?

Then you tell me because life is how you made it for us, and you didn't even have to do that much. Then I realized that we don't deserve a way back to you, but you loved us so much that you gave us your son to show us the way back to you. All I have and anyone else has to do is claim it.

Thank you, God, for giving me what I need when I need it and not what I want when I want it. Your plans and ideas come out far greater than my ideas. I want to serve you better than I have been. I want to give you my whole heart in worship, and I want to give you all of the praise I have given in my life. It's all of yours in the first place. You know my heart, God. I love you for that. Please help and guide me through your will, and never let me go alone. I want and need you to guide me as my savior, Jesus.

3 AM Again!

I am awake at 3 AM and not writing long, but I wanted to thank God for the music he has put into my life. I had a song pop in my head about wiping away stains as I saw a water stain. Then another song came into my head as I turned, saw the clock on the microwave say "3 AM", and turned again to see my journal waiting for me to write in it again as though God was telling me to get going. And so I did. Thanks be to God for everything in my life!

5 PM

Yesterday, I met with my attorney and my previous employer, who fired me for making a mistake. I followed my lawyer's advice and tried to move on with my life. During this time, I wrote a book and accepted that I might not receive anything from the lawsuit.

The meeting was extremely difficult and tiring. They tried to refute every argument I presented, but I could sense their unease when asking questions as I told them nothing but the truth. Their questions made me feel they knew more about me than I did.

I hadn't acted out in two weeks but was still thinking about it. I wasn't sure if my behavior was healthy or a compulsion, so I planned to bring it up with my therapist during our next session. I couldn't understand why the lawyers wanted my journal documents. It felt like they thought I might harm someone in the same way they harmed me. I was worried about a few things in my case, and I wondered how much longer it would go on.

I want my acting-out behavior to end, but I have come so far not to give up. I needed to endure and wait through this process, and justice would serve its purpose. I prayed that it would be a win for me. Either way, I feel proud of my endurance to last throughout that time. I couldn't have made it to the other side if I had endured it any sooner. God, thank you for bringing me through to this point and beyond.

I sought God's assistance in continuing my journey towards the end of that challenging period. Despite my dislike for fast food, I cherished the company of my friends there in recovery. Their words of encouragement and innovative ideas were helpful for my progress. Although I was doing well, I remained cautious of anyone who tried to bring me down or hinder my progress.

With God's help, I was confident I could tackle any obstacle. I was grateful for the Creator's mighty hands and trusted His ability to help me overcome any challenge. Thank you, God!

I am angry at my attorney for dropping the case. He dropped it because he might lose, but I am frustrated that I listened to my pastor for giving me advice I now feel I shouldn't have taken. I feel angry at myself for listening to my heart early on and not following through with the lawsuit in the first place. Most importantly, I am frustrated at you, God!

I received a call from a recruiter for a gas station and general store job. I have an opportunity to work for a company with strong Christian roots. One day, people will know me for something great—a purpose for God that brings people back to the morals and humanized ways of life that God had planned for us initially.

I once met a young girl who seemed clueless about life. She was a friend of my dopey friend. She appeared lost, yet she didn't even know she was lost. She had heard of Jesus but knew little about him or what he had done. She also had little knowledge about God. I hoped that my friend wouldn't scare her away with his sexual advances and that she would find her way in life.

He calls her his sister, but I see more than that in his eyes for her. I see a lot of my old self in my dopey friend, which scares me, too. I want to help others like him out so much—because of what I have become. It is time to tell the rest of my story.

Yesterday's worship was such a blessing from God that it made me cry tears of joy. For the first time in years, I saw my old friend, who had become a pastor. I asked him to please pray for me. I had been feeling lost and alone for some time now. I felt like my spiritual mentor had abandoned me, and he showed me so much love and compassion that it could only have come from the Holy Spirit.

It truly was love from God. The encounter with my friend rekindled something I hadn't felt for a long time. I thank God for my friend and his family, who have been such a blessing to my life. His presence alone was an answer to a prayer.

Lord, you are using my friend to help me move past my old self. Because of my friend's obedient heart, you have blessed my life at this moment. I hope to hear back from my Mother in Christ and her family. She is truly my spiritual mother, and I would probably be dead if God hadn't placed her in my life.

God, thank you for a blessed day yesterday. Please use me and teach me how you want me to be so that I can be what you need of me each day as I live here on earth. Amen!

I had an interview with an insurance company in the heart of downtown. It went well, as did all of my interviews. However, I am worried about not getting my A+ certification before the hire date. I passed the test in 1998 but lost my certificate, so I had to retake it.

My wife and I let a girl stay with us after my dopey friend met up with her and tried to take advantage of her. He failed due to our efforts, and we told her about his HIV issues. We found out that he didn't tell her anything about the issue and that he was selling his medications to other people on the street downtown.

That same dopey friend called me later in the day to ask me for a ride, only to hear him asking someone if they wanted one of his pills in the background of the call. I have been so upset about a lot of things lately. I don't know how to regain control of my life and beat this addiction. Right now, I feel like asking my new roommates for a threesome. It is something I haven't experienced yet. Not that I want to hurt my wife, but I want to experience the rush of the high of such a thing, and I don't know why.

This is my last chance. Why have I kept my thoughts to myself, only to have them all come out now? Am I awake now, God? Or am I still in my fantasy world? I keep hurting others, and it doesn't stop. Why am I holding back? Why can't I let things go?

The biggest secret I've kept from my wife is that my parents disapproved of her when we first met. They are a large part of my pain and anger growing up. I need to let it all go. Deep down, I knew my thoughts and feelings had been wrong, but I didn't know how to stop them. The pain I've caused others has shown me the need to let go of my feelings and start over.

I am no longer abused! My brother can't hurt me anymore! My cousins can't abuse me in the middle of my sleep. I don't need to be afraid of the dark. I wouldn't say I liked the things I had done. They are eating away at my soul. I know what I did was wrong now, and I must repent. Today, I love myself, and I love my wife. I need her as my partner in life. I am no longer that hurt boy.

The people who claim to be my friends but don't come around aren't my friends, and neither are those who force me to love someone else. I now need to learn what love is for real, and that isn't sex or physical attention but the most powerful emotion of life.

I had a tough day at work. A lot of thinking was going on in my head. I was grateful to speak with one of the female roommates' caseworkers about her medications. She needs something to help her cope with whatever is hurting her. I know I won't be trying anything with her anytime soon, and I hope she does better today and in the future. Otherwise, I must put my foot down and make her leave.

As far as my addiction is concerned, I want to act out with her in my mind, but my heart is telling me not to. I have lived inside my head for a long time, but I am finally listening to my heart. I still haven't heard from my former mentoring pastor. I am not sure if I should see her or not.

Dear Past Self,

How are you doing today? I am worried about where you need to go next. I hope you are feeling better than in days past. I know that the addiction has been dragging you down, and we have been able to fantasize about past escorts and flings like the girl we are sharing the apartment with.

I know you are unsure how to deal with your past, so writing a letter to yourself might be a good way to change your self-talk. It can heal you and help you regain control of your life.

One thing I wanted to say to you was that I love you, and I pray for you to get over your past abuse. I want us to work together and be a whole person again. It seems silly that I am writing a letter like this to the child inside of me, but I am willing to try anything at this point to get over my past abusive mindset.

I want us both to become the best version of ourselves. I won't give up until we are healed and living in the present. I don't want to live in the past any longer. What happened in the past wasn't our fault. We can let it go together.

One day, it was the right thing to do now. By that, I mean writing a letter to myself in the past. That said, I hope it isn't crazy of me to do such a thing. It was a good idea at the time and an excellent way to talk to myself about my past problems.

You are not alone in this battle. You are safe with me beside you. If you or I have any feelings to deal with, let's write them out instead of holding them in and acting out with prostitutes and escorts. Deal?

This is the most I have written to anyone in a long time, but I can come up with more now as I continue not to allow my brain to argue with me anymore. I am sure you will agree that this is a good and healthy way for us to get over the abuse from our past. This will allow us to grow where we need to succeed.

I hope it will bring out the best and lose the chains that have bound us to the behaviors. All of those beatings we took so long ago, the sexual abuse endured by so many people, I hope they all become healed.

Those people can't hurt us now, but we will overcome this with God's help. God will get us out of this. All we need to do is let go and forgive those who have hurt us. Pray that their suffering will end and that God will show us how to love like him.

I know you love me. I can tell by the actions you are taking now. You are trying everything to improve, and I am proud of you. Let's keep taking those steps together and let God's love hold us up. Let us show the world how he first loved us. With all the love in my heart,

Your Future Self

Dear Older Self,

I can see myself as a 12-year-old kid now. I also think it's crazy that I am writing back to my future self-replies, but if the issues are resolved, so be it. There are a couple of reasons why I am stuck here. A couple of things happened at this age in my life.

First, my brother went into the military, and my dad went into the hospital for pancreatitis surgery. I have lost a lot of years thinking about the miracle that God did in bringing my father back from the dead. It still seems like yesterday that it all happened. This is why I have recurring dreams of him being alive now. I can't see him gone from this world. I also think that this was the age at which I got into a fight with a bully at my school.

I was the bully by calling a kid's girlfriend a few rude names. I can't remember her last name, but I can still picture her face and the faces of the other people in that room as I stabbed her with my words. It plays back in my mind as though I was just there. Many things happened to me that year, and it amazes me that I lived through it all.

I know I can fade in and out of time in the memories of my past. I see a lot of what I remember from then was how much abuse I took from friends who weren't friends at all. The people I cared most about weren't there to protect and care for me, and they didn't tell me what I went through was terrible. It was also when I first abused my nephew.

I was trying to grasp my abuse at my brother's hands. My nephew described how someone else had shown him how to have sex, and I took advantage of the opportunity to continue the same behaviors as my brother. In my heart, I knew it was my brother who had done such a thing. And I wanted to know why. So I did the same thing that was done to me.

I want to let the past stuff go, but it is where all of the action was in my life at the time, and it is hard to let it all go in any case. I need help letting it all go, but I want to know if you or I are strong enough to handle it ourselves. I want to trust that you won't let me down anymore. I know that you have been broken a lot as well. We have done a lot of work to get to this point of healing. I want you to keep your end up as well.

I know it will be challenging, but we are starting to make it out of the darkness and into the light. I can tell you are sincere about getting better. I want to hold on to something like my dad's defying death that one time forever. How could I ever replace that memory? I am afraid of getting out of my past because it is there; my dad is still alive and strong.

Most of all, he was there to protect me. I don't know how to continue to defend myself with those who tried to protect me being gone. That said, let's work on protecting ourselves from future abuse.

Respectfully yours,
Future Self

I had a wonderful walk tonight. The clouds looked like I was staring right at heaven. The higher portion of the clouds was glowing, resembling sunshine on a wall of thinly lined clouds. The view seemed like the world had stopped in its tracks, giving me a glimpse of the edge of where it stopped. Then, on the other side, heaven beamed with golden sun rays, showing the wall and gates of heaven.

Then, I came home to the aftermath of my addictive thoughts. This time, my sinful thoughts made me want to return for another peaceful walk with God. My addiction seems to be getting worse instead of better, though. I was told that I said my wife was fat, and I don't remember that I said anything of the sort. I could probably say anything in my addictive mindset once it gets triggered.

I had a great session with my therapist today, but I didn't follow through with most of his advice until My wife intervened. I am glad that I walked instead of relieving myself in other ways. I am still overwhelmed after my walk, but I think that's because I walked right back into the chaos I created earlier with my addictive mind. I feel like I have been losing my battles with addiction for so long that I haven't let God in to do his part.

For all of that, I am very displeased with myself. I can keep the promise that God will be there for me when I need him, but is that enough? If only he could strike this female roommate mute, that would be awesome. I was kidding, God!

God,

I am feeling frustrated with the girl who is living with us. She doesn't seem to be interested in getting better and makes up excuses to avoid taking her medications. Moreover, she argues with everyone who tries to guide her on improving her health or abstaining from certain things. It's becoming increasingly difficult to deal with her behavior.

I feel like I have no control over my emotions around this girl. She often behaves like a three-year-old, and her boyfriend always takes her side, even when she's wrong. He's a coward, and his lack of willingness to confront her on her behavior will eventually lead to problems. However, I am thankful that God has put me in this position to learn how to handle these situations and manage my emotions, including my anger.

On the second day, our new female roommate took her medications. She hasn't called to bother me at work about any nonsense. Her medications are helping to keep her moods under control, and she seems down to earth for now.

My day has been great and uneventful. Yesterday, we all went to the park and played with a Frisbee. We all seemed to have a lot of fun, and I didn't see any change in her mood, even when I accidentally hit her in the head with the Frisbee. I got a lot of things done today at work. I want a pill that will fix it all and make life better.

It is getting easier to write in my journal, but on Sunday, I found myself out of control. I am not sure why I started lying and trying to get sexual with a girl I had met online. She was asking me for advice on how to pronounce words in English, but I wanted to vent and lose myself in my addiction.

I got caught up even worse in the moment than I think I might have done before. I lied to my wife and a friend from my support group. I came to my senses yesterday and told the truth. I left my shame and humbled myself by sharing what was on my mind and what I almost did. I need to remind myself to keep my eyes on my paper. I want a pill to make me better and move on from my addiction.

I had a rough time at work. I am not sure why I was at my wit's end with my addictive behaviors. I could have been caught at work talking and sexting this woman from Australia. I sent her a video of me masturbating in the restroom stall at work. How sick is that? I am getting more and more powerless over my actions every day. I am doing less and less work. It's like I am tired of my job. I can't stay focused, and I keep turning to a site for chatting with others about depression and anxiety. I thought it might have helped me out, but I will be damned if I am not finding myself trailing off to other sites and rooms to chat in them to look for women.

Even now, I feel lost. The words I am writing should have taken the entire page, but I am only halfway through. I keep losing interest in life and heading back to my fantasy world. I don't know if my losses are causing this or if my thoughts about life are cutting me down at the knees. I need help staying focused and busy at work.

I am afraid my addictive behavior is going to show up sooner or later again at work. I don't know what else to do other than to try and stay off the sites. I need to keep myself from chat rooms altogether forever.

What used to be easy for me has become more challenging to do. I don't know how to return to where I was before I went off the rails. I truly feel lost. I need help getting out. I need help getting back to my old self again. I feel like my addictive mind is winning the short battle right now.

Today has been a good day. I got a lot done at work, I was able to focus, and I was free from my addiction for the day. While the temptation was there, it didn't provoke me to the point it did yesterday, and I feel very relieved about it. Even a daily reading today struck a chord with me.

The reading gave me hope that I don't have to try and change the world, but instead, I need to change what I can control and leave the world to its ways of directing sexuality. My thoughts don't have to be the same as the world's, but I should fiercely protect myself from the people, places, and things that might trigger me to relapse back into my behaviors. Easier said than done.

Dear God,

Thank you for bringing me back to the present today. Thank you for bringing me out of my addictive mindset. Please don't let me go down that road again. Please don't let me go down to that darkness of my addictive behaviors. Help strengthen my heart and mind to fight this behavior issue I am struggling with. Please show me how to follow you each day of my life.

I want to thank you, God, for everything you continually do for me. Even when things seem inadequate, you know what is happening. You have total control over the situation. You have total control over my whole life. Please let me participate when I need to learn something, but love me as you always do when I don't learn the lesson.

I know you have what's best for me in store, and I accept that today. I know you will have the same results tomorrow, too. Thank you for loving me every day of my life.

You are truly good to me. With love back,
Your Humble Servant!

Today, I had a great session with my therapist. Then, he gave me some coping skill ideas on a worksheet. He gave me a sheet that had anxiety exercises for dealing with my problems. One thing I just realized I need to deal with is the idea of someone tickling me hurts me physically and mentally.

I feel pain when someone tickles me. It is also an emotional pain to be tickled. It brings back up the thought of the abuse I went through. It hurts me and stops me in my tracks. It keeps me from functioning mentally and turns me into a nine-year-old boy again. I could see it happening this time in my mind. It made me instantly scared and feel defensive towards others.

I know for most people, tickling can be a good thing, but for an abused person, it was a way for my family to control and manipulate me. It was a form of torture in my mind. It brought my mind back to the abuse whenever my wife tickled me. It was a bit of a breakthrough, but I still need to work on it. That's one down and many to go.

I forgot about writing this down when it happened last night, but my wife left to house-sit. It took a while, but I eventually felt lost and scared without her. I was lost at the old clothing store with the elephant slide and the playground in the back. It was where parents took their children in the 80s to play while they shopped.

My parents needed to find out where I had gone off to every time we went to that store. I could picture myself climbing the big underbelly of the elephant slide and looking out the eyes to see the shoppers. I could slide down its mouth and see many parents waiting for their kids. I always seemed to run ahead of my parents and forget about the worries of abuse in those times. I only realized I was lost once the store got dark. Then, I cried out for my mom and dad.

Today, church stunk, and I felt I got nothing out of it. I asked our music director if I could lead a worship service at the mid-point group. She asked if I could look up some verses about Paul and his struggles, and I agreed. I would then send her what I would preach about and see where that went.

I feel like they think I am lacking in Godly love, but I am praying that God will come down on my soul and make me whole again to the point that I can listen to his word for my life and blow them all away. I know I don't say much in the band, and I have taken a back seat to the worship service lately, but I think that was because I needed to heal from my self-inflicted abuse. I know in my heart I am getting better every day. Today, I am breaking free from sin with the help of Jesus Christ, my Lord and Savior. Amen!

Last night was fantastic! Five thousand plus men singing. During Lincoln Brewster, we heard Hallelujah, and I was in Heaven. A tremendous guitar solo set the tone for me during the entire conference. Writing in a folding chair in a noisy stadium full of guys is hard. I want to help men find God, continue to live for God, and carve his word into my heart—a captive audience with few vendors. I have not seen anyone talk about abuse, but so much towards healing and saving.

I have finally found a group that potentially deals with adults who have been sexually abused as children for support. Then, an old fling reappeared, to my dismay, and brought back some resentment for me. Not that I don't like her, but that she is blinded by several things in her life. She refuses to see that her life is in ruins without Christ in it.

I refuse to force it down her throat, but she needs help, and that is how I feel called to help her. I just found out that her daughter is trying to put her away for assault. I am glad I got rid of drama from my life with the female roommate and her boyfriend, but sometimes I miss drama.

I want to text a girl I met at a bar to see if she will help me act out and give me that high feeling I crave. I don't know why I like it. All I get out of these situations is trouble. I should talk about that in my group tonight. Another thing I am worried about is that Celebrate Recovery is the only group dealing with the issues I am having with my past abuse. We will see.

Even in Celebrate Recovery, the issues of abuse are only focused on women and not on men. Again, it all continues to feel hopeless. I wonder why no one is dealing with the real issues of abuse in men. The men of the world seem to be getting told to suck it up and remain silent about their past abuse, even here. Their left wall shows scripture in Hebrew John 7:37. Their right wall shows scripture in Greek John 11:25.

I started writing something on Tuesday but stopped because I was distracted. I'm unsure if I should respond to the new music director's email. I feel like he is being a colossal bully towards me, but at the same time, maybe it's God's way of telling me to focus on my abuse ministry entirely.

One thing I know is definitely that I am not alone in this. Even if people aren't talking about it here, I know I can talk about it in other places, and I can destroy the silence surrounding abuse for all men. I know what they went through because I went through it, too.

I find it scarier to face the reality of how many people are being hurt by abuse than to stop and let someone else handle it. What's even worse is the knowledge that some people are choosing to ignore the issue and, in turn, are hurting others who may be suffering in silence.

I find it difficult not to objectify women, especially when they are dressed in revealing clothing. However, I believe that this behavior reflects their desire for power rather than just being a male behavior. My goal is to make a positive impact on this issue. Additionally, I need to work on finding healthier ways to love and express myself instead of relying on sexual behavior.

Today was pretty uneventful, but I can imagine it was tragic, too. I am scared of writing for some reason. After my dad died, I haven't written much as compared to my past notes in my journal. I did go online today and figured out that there was a place where unhealthy men went to think that they were getting healthy for themselves. One even mentioned that I did not involve God in my recovery messages, but I let them know where I stood. God is a loving being, and there was no way for me to leave God out. He is everything to my recovery. Leaving God out of my life would be like living without air. God is above all, is in all, and is a part of my recovery as I go through life.

I can't explain the love God has shown me over the years in words alone. He shows it through the people, places, and events in my life. Sometimes good, sometimes bad, but always for the best of what goes on in my life.

Sometimes, I worry, though, that my life doesn't matter or that what I think doesn't count towards anything good to the cause of childhood sexual abuse survivors or sexual addiction, for that matter. I am probably preparing myself for failure in those thoughts, so I must stop that "stinkin' thinkin'." I hope I can twelve-step someone into our group tonight, but life will continue even if we don't. I hope that my Recovery Mentor gets here soon.

Today, I realized just how powerless I can be over my addictive mindset. The idea that I can act out at any given time scares me, and I wonder just how much I can keep myself from wanting the temptation to go ahead and act on it. One thing I am apprehensive about is that I now have money to spend in my own savings account.

My mind keeps wanting to go there and spend it on an escort. I want to save the money to give my wife an exceptional vacation. That will be a better choice of what to do with the money. Now, my mind is trying to convince me it is alright to act out with the money I have saved. It keeps saying it is only one time. Then, it will start up again in the next pay period, saving more money. I need to see my psychiatrist. I am unsure what else to say other than I am tempted and need to call someone to discuss this.

I was frustrated with a request that was due to be mine in the work queue. It had been there for over a month and was a mass migration request. I was not aware of it or that I needed to handle it, which made me feel frustrated and angry. But I know there is a God, and I am not Him.

I am very bored and lonely right now. I should listen to music, but I also want something to do. I found out I can navigate to the escort pages of the Dark Web because our blocker here at work only blocks the acceptance statement page. If I navigate to the city and add the female escort subtext, I can still access the ads. This is not good for my addiction. I am going to talk about this in a group tonight.

Sex addiction is only found in the shadow of death! I need to learn how to be in a relationship. Sex without love is only found in the shadow of death. There is a god, and I am not God, but God is in me.

3:30 AM

There is a song about a man who wakes up at 3 AM and has to start writing what's on his heart. So, he writes about God and what God has done in his life. God has done some very amazing miracles in my life up to this point. He has done everything to help comfort me; even more than that, he has given me hope and a new life. Last night at the Christmas Eve service, something clicked in my heart. I felt alive in a new way. It was like how the Bible described new life. I can't describe it other than love and peace, which are the only things that come to my mind how I feel.

Helping my friends and family has been a dream of mine for a long time. I am especially looking out for my new female friend and the dopey boy she picked up. Yep, he is back in my life again.

This time, he needed help with other things, like a place to stay and help with getting around. While he is currently in jail, and I know he feels alone, I pray that God will calm his heart and use his life for a greater purpose. God has something up his sleeve for my dopey friend that is transpiring; only God knows how it will end. Even this dopey friend of mine has a purpose in life, and I, for one, look forward to seeing what is in the sight of God's great purpose.

I thank God for bringing the two of them into my life, and I know that something good will come out of helping them in their walk and giving them hope to be better people in the eyes of God. My dopey friend has the love of God in his heart buried deep within him, and the same can be said of his new girlfriend.

I felt the same love when I studied under my first mentor. I also pray for my wife to find peace in her heart tonight. I know she is hurting because of my actions, and I am responsible for her aggravation. I love my wife very much. She has helped me more than anyone else in my life. She is a true believer and a solid rock in Christ Jesus. Amen!

I don't know where to begin. My day has been so mixed up, and right now, I feel angry at my wife for not allowing me to finish having sex with her last night. I am angry at myself for falling into lustful thoughts about other women, and I feel like I need to divorce her.

I don't want to, but my head is lost in a cloud of selfishness and a desire to help others. I am not helping anyone by doing what I am doing right now. I wish my wife could see the world as I see it, but I don't know if anyone can. I feel lost and alone because she would rather spend all her time watching television or on her phone.

She doesn't want to play video games, go for walks, or even tell me how she feels. She doesn't show me any emotions other than anger and hatred towards the goals I am setting. She seems bitter towards my love for helping others, or she is angry at me for finding empathy for women who sell themselves to make a living.

I don't know what I am doing, but I know that I am hurting other people, including my wife, who I think still loves me. My ADD is causing a great separation from my heart as well as from my mind. I want to feel normal. I want to live life to its fullest. What that might mean is up for interpretation. It depends on how we want to live life, right? God, I am scared of what will happen next in my life. Do I ask for the divorce or leave it alone?

As if I couldn't make things any worse, I managed to make them even more amplified.

In my power, I couldn't get away from the addiction. The power of sin had me to the point of pain, and I wasn't able to go anywhere. Locking me up and throwing away the key was all I could hear in my mind. Was my first therapist correct in her evaluation? Maybe she was right, and there was no hope for me. Do I leave everyone and go off and be alone?

In 2013, a new couple joined the church family. They were coming back to the area and heard about our pastor and his wacky ways of loving people. The man quickly became a good friend and mentor. He was older and more in tune with God than I was then. He had a similar story to mine with sex addiction and homosexual tendencies. He managed to break free from his behaviors, and I wanted to know his secrets.

His wife had been diagnosed with cancer several times throughout their married life, and they could never have children. It was almost a mirrored scenario of my wife and I's relationship. They adopted a boy when they were young after finding out that they couldn't have children, but I was not ready to adopt someone else's children for fear of my past coming back to bite me or putting a child in harm's way. My wife and I both wanted children, but only if God was going to bring us to them.

One day, I asked him to mentor me in what brought him freedom from the sexual sins he was facing, and he brought me to a program he found online that helped him beat sexual sin. Only the program he brought me to wasn't about sexual sin at all. He noticed something else was a deeper issue I was facing that was keeping me trapped in my sin.

I had been promoting my book Bigger Than Me for some time, but he noticed that I had another issue that went much deeper and could be the underlying cause of my behaviors. He saw right through the lying. He noticed that I couldn't get away from the idea that medications weren't helping to keep my behavior at bay. He noticed that I was getting worse instead of better, no matter how hard I tried. He recommended I go through the Cross-Centered Mind course rather than the sexual addiction course at "Setting Captives Free." So I agreed to start the process, only to find out it was a course to help people get away from mental health drugs and medications.

"I didn't have a problem with mental health medications." I thought to myself. "They were helping me fight my addiction!" I explained to him how the doctors said I shouldn't go off of them or I could have worse problems. He encouraged me to stay the course. These next few chapters are about how God used me to humble the medical industry by freeing me from my behaviors and mental health medications.

Chapter 12

2014 - 2015

Setting Captives Free

"THEREFORE IF ANYONE IS IN CHRIST, HE IS A NEW CREATURE; THE OLD THINGS PASSED AWAY; BEHOLD, NEW THINGS HAVE COME." 2 CORINTHIANS 5:17 NASB

11:57 AM

I haven't been thinking about God or giving him all my attention. I can see I have a lot missing in my life, but nothing I can do will change that until I give up my will and let God do the work he needs to do inside me.

I spoke with my accountability partner about what I tried to get at. He showed me that I was only fooling myself into thinking

I knew God's word and was not in it often enough. I was fooling myself into thinking I was giving God praise, but I was still being selfish in my own heart.

I pray that God will continue to work in my life. I pray for change in my perspective of living each day. I pray God brings my life back to follow him closely and that He will address the issues I need to work on. As my newfound mentor pointed out, I pray that God will be there when I must address them.

Another prayer I need to pray is that God help me better understand what a good husband is and how I need to be a better husband. I also need God to help me change how I treat my wife. I need to be a better husband and not be who I have been most of the time these past several years.

With my dad gone now, I have had to step up, and I have been afraid to do so thus far. I felt he was always here and never left, and I remained a child. I have let this part of my life tear me up for far too long. I need to address it with God, and I need to come to terms with the fact that my dad is gone from this side of heaven.

Dad,

I love and miss you very much, but I want to be led deeper into God's presence, and I need to let you go to God's care now. I know you will be safe with God and always in my heart. Amen!

2:35 AM

I started a new raspberry ketone dietary supplement. How is it working? I do know that God is working in me today. I have been taking an online course called The Cross-centered Mind, and God has shown himself to me in many ways. Not that I should go into ministry, but that I am already in the ministry field with where I am today.

God's word has been making me a better person each day. With God's help, I have been able to set boundaries, which are saving my life and my marriage. I finally realize I have limited time here and must care for what God has given me. I can't take care of anything else. I need to leave those other things up to God to handle. I still have thoughts and doubts about what I should keep doing and abstain from. I believe I am right where God wants me to be now.

God has been holding onto me this entire time, loving me far more than I could have ever known. I still wonder where I am going next, but I know God will lead the way as I ask him for guidance.

God is like a mother, inside the Holy Spirit, inside me. A mother shows us that the world can be a safe and loving place, but she also shows us that it can be dangerous if we cross certain lines. That same Holy Spirit can guide our hearts if we listen.

The Holy Spirit encourages me to go one step further than I did the day before. I feel like I can do anything today except live without God in my life. I am not sure where I am going with this, but I do know that as it is now, God is leading me, and I trust Him more than I trust myself.

I can now feel the prayers of my past coming to be and working on my life. This week, I learned that prayer is more than a feeling of want or a wish; it is a place to share your deepest desires and listen to God speak to your heart through the help of the Holy Spirit.

I am not sure where I am at today. I am fighting the urge to act out, but I know I can't do that because I have already tried and lost that money to an ugly drug-addicted hooker. I didn't even release. I felt like crap after that. Am I giving in to my addiction, or maybe I am getting better about feeling guilty about my actions and the shame of it all?

As I am going through the muck of my past and the family environment that I grew up in, I feel a great deal of anxiety and stress. I want my wife to have sex with me like she used to. Even that has changed in our relationship. I am fantasizing about this other girl. I would like to have her for fun but not for anything else. She is cute in my mind and imagination, but deep down, I know she is a person. I feel the same way towards my wife right now.

I hope that my wife will have me again. I would like that more than anything else I have done in the past. I want to believe I won't do it again, but I know I will. I also have issues with my past and present morals. I feel so messed up, with feelings of loneliness and untrustworthiness.

I want to influence others, but I find myself acting out like the rest of the world. I want to control my impulses and behaviors, but the actions I have been taking are so numbing my heart and exciting my brain to act out with other people. I like sex more than anything else in the world right now. I remember how I could always tell myself I was good at it growing up. It was my coping skill. Now, it is a death trap. God! Please get me out!

I am feeling very alone and in a very dark place today. Last night, I was more destructive than ever before. My heart was hurting because I didn't feel understood by people. I was lost last night, and I wanted someone to find me.

I still feel the same way this morning. If that girl would ask today to sleep with me, I would act on it. This is her only day to act on it. After today, I am done acting out. I am going to stick to my boundaries. I need to lose the money I have been giving myself to put back into our checking account for safekeeping. It ends here and now.

God knows I have lust in my heart and that I lost my way. God didn't lose my way. I lost my way and need to grow up and care for myself. No one else will do that, not even my wife. Not to sound mean by that, but I mean that only I know how to care for myself. Except for God, no one else knows better about my wants and needs than I do.

I need to go to God more daily because His view of my life is perfect. He can see further ahead and knows what will happen before I do. I need to trust in that promise and allow God to lead my life instead of telling God how I want to live. I want to live for others, but I have to live for myself first and stop what I am doing.

Please help me abstain from my bad behaviors, learn to love myself and others better, and take better care of myself. I love my wife so much, but I am losing myself to sin and shame. Point me back to where you want me to go: with love for myself and others, morals, and integrity. I need to be grounded in you, God. Please help me rise and be changed for your glory. Amen!

Yesterday was both disturbing and eye-opening. I acted out again at work because I was frustrated at another employee and bored. I had a huge lack of support from my teammates to finish work. I blame myself for acting out without reason other than anger towards others, which is a huge problem for me.

On the other hand, I am feeling better today because I decided to go to my recovery meeting and spill my guts about acting out at work. I asked the group for assistance addressing my feelings and observing what they saw in my actions. I was in a very dark place when I acted out and needed their input. I had scared myself to the point of acting out with a vengeance because I act out when I am scared, too.

A member explained to me a problem that he saw I had. He explained that I was looking for a reason to act out and not for a solution to stop acting out. He further explained that I needed to give my addictive behaviors up to God and not look for an excuse but for a reason not to act out. I only need to focus on what I can do and lose the reason why I do what I do. I should stay focused on abstaining rather than on why I do it.

While I might still have these urges, I still want to know why I do the acting out. I know focusing on the why is causing me more harm than good. So, for today, at least, I am staying sober and making amends for others and myself. Thanks be to God! Amen.

I knew something was wrong. I knew that God had a plan for my life, but I also worried about not knowing what that plan was. I didn't want to worry about it anymore. I knew I shouldn't worry about what God had in store for my life, but this fear was a reverent fear more than a worry. My goal in the hospital came from the course I have been working in, "The Cross Centered Mind" course. It was to get off of all of my mental health and ADD medications. We will see how well this works.

Yesterday, I checked myself into the mental health hospital's inpatient care in hopes of getting my medications under control. I have been having anxiety attacks, trimmers, and thoughts about hurting myself and others. Not that I would act on those thoughts of harming myself, but that I have a problem with feeling suicidal.

I have a problem with feeling suicidal because God has instilled it in my heart to enjoy life, and my dad has also raised me to show that life has value and suicide is a cop-out. I knew this thought came from outside of me, and I was done arguing with demons.

Last night, my wife forgot to bring in my bible. At first, I was angry with her for forgetting to bring my bible to read, but then I found comfort in knowing God put my heart at ease by seeing two names written in a Gideon bible on a bookshelf in the mental hospital and their phone numbers in the

Bible as well. My pastor and one of my friends, who was a regular at the hospital, were written in the bible.

What a weird sign from God! I know now that this is where I need to be. It was like God placed me without a bible to go to the bookshelf to find this one. I later learned that my friend accidentally left the Bible there on his last visit. I know that God is truly watching over me here, and when I leave this place, He will still be with me.

Yesterday, I met a young lady in the hospital. She was 34 years old and very caring towards others but didn't love herself very much. She was a lot like me. She has put herself in danger in hopes of meeting new friends. Her relationships had all but taken her spirit away. I have been praying for her every day since meeting her, and when I get out, I will continue to pray for her to be healed. I wanted to get her a birthday gift and maybe a party. I didn't know her birth date. I will have to ask her if I see her again.

Today, I am feeling better, but I am still having issues with anxiety and depression. I wanted to go home but was angry that the nursing staff hadn't gotten the food I ordered. At least I am writing about it instead of beating the old lady's head. She couldn't read an order to save her life. I have been worried about the ability to want still to act out.

I am at a point in my Cross-centered Mind program where they want me to get off the medications I am taking for depression and anxiety. They are partnered with a program called The Road Back program. They help people get off of psychiatric medications. This is the biggest reason I came into the inpatient care program at the mental health hospital.

The doctors here aren't listening to me about the Road Back Program. I am not sure what to believe in anymore. The program wants me to wean off the medications, and I think I want to do that as well, but the doctors won't listen to me here. I pray that they will listen to me a little better and help me go through what I asked of them originally. We will see.

3:07 AM

I am awake as usual at 3 AM with my restroom romp. I feel like I had sex with my wife for the first time in 10 years, and it was amazing to feel loved again. I am beginning to think the medications had everything to do with my acting out behaviors, but I still am thinking about other people I have been with. Still, it isn't sticking in my head like it used to while I was on the medications. So far, so good. Things are coming around, and good things are coming from this, and I am starting to love myself again.

I don't know if I am feeling anything now. My heart feels like it is gone. My mind feels like it is gone, and I feel like I want to hurt myself. I feel alone and without any recourse. I could lose my wife, my job, and my friends all in one big shit-hole gamble. This is my lowest point today. I can't even remember what I did other than I acted out, and it ruined me this time because it caused me to lie, cheat, steal, harm a loved one, and glutton after something I had no idea was so horrible. I didn't even know something so horrible could even exist. I truly feel nothing right now, but at the same time, I feel free.

I am also feeling dead to the world. I should be dead after what I had done. What I did felt like a dream; I would wake up from it at any moment and realize that nothing happened. Then the horrible feelings would all rush back into my body, and all of it would go away, and it would all just be a dream.

This morning, I forgot the keys in the car, and I thought I had lost them. I now feel like I lost my soul. I'm not completely off of all of my medications yet, but I am darn close. I hope I can make it out alive. I am so sick of my addiction that I stole a computer from work to get sex with a prostitute who looked like she was barely 18. This disease is going to kill me if I don't stop now. I feel like I just lost my wife for good.

One question I still have around all of this is once I get off from all of the medications, will there still be a life to live, or will I be alone to destroy myself further? I have let everyone down now. My wife, mother, family, friends, mentors, and myself. The hardest thing to understand is I don't know why I did any of it. My heart feels like it is gone. It is all gone, almost as if everyone abandoned me.

My body feels alive and free for the first time. I feel safe with my wife lying outside our bed, and it won't matter. This is my final time acting out! I plan to keep a journal of my way back to God, and I feel free for the first time in a long time in my life. I think maybe it took God hitting me over the head with the car door to make me see what I was doing wrong.

Previously, my thoughts would make most people sick to their stomachs. I had yet to convince myself I had changed, but I will improve starting today. I feel 100% better getting off the medication than I have ever felt while being on the medications. I am almost off them now; I know I could quit them soon. I feel like the medications were holding me down and keeping me stuck in my addiction. Only time will tell, and only God knows. God deserves all of the credit for this.

I finally heard back from the friend who owned the bible. I am not sure yet what happened to him, but he tried to get off of his medications again, and he became out of control. He went into hiding for about four months. I was glad to hear back from him today. It gave me some fear that what I was doing might not be the right thing to do, seeing him suffer.

God, however, has given me lots of hope throughout my journey that my life can and will change if I follow the good example He has set for me. It won't be easy because of the people I face daily, but I will see that my side of the road stays clean. I still feel tempted to spend money on escorts and other stupid things, but I have managed to avoid that fiasco for now.

It has been a month since I last acted out with an escort. While I still feel like acting out, I can finally tell myself I don't need to. While that is a good feeling, it is still a worrying point for me. I worry that those thoughts will still torment me into acting out in the future.

I look forward to getting healthier than I have been, but I am also very cautious about what isn't God's plan and what God wants me to get back in line with for my life. I need to get back to finish my course-work with Setting Captives Free online, and I need to start working on my fourth step in recovery. These things will teach me much about myself and who I have become.

Getting off from mental health medications was one of the hardest things to do in my life. I had nightmares, night sweats, brain fog, and moments where I wanted to harm myself badly. It wasn't for the faint of heart. I continued the behaviors until I was off the medications, but My mentor friend who brought me to the Cross-centered Mind course was right.

The course and The Road-back program online helped me withdraw with few side effects. Some people report brain zapping, but I never had those effects. Others reported deeper hallucinations, but I managed to dodge those effects. I was becoming free for the first time in over 10 years of mental health prognosis. Doctors couldn't believe it. My doctor even said that if I felt depression again or anxiety, they could put me back on the medications. I ran out of that room quicker than anyone could care to stop me.

Today is the last day of medications. I have told the doctors I will no longer be taking any of the medications I was on for depression, anxiety, Adult ADD, and stress. God has freed me, and I am ready to move on, free from shame. I no longer hear voices in my mind telling me to act out. I am no longer feeling the cravings to be with other women. What did they put in my drink for the past 12 years?

I have a lot of things going on in my head right now, and I am still trying to figure out where to start. I should start by praying for guidance and wisdom from God first. I haven't been alone with myself for some time now. I last wrote in my journal in May. I am still free from the medications, but something is still missing.

I am free, but now that I have escaped that prison, I am becoming more under attack than I have ever felt while on the medications. A lot has happened since I came off the medications. My hand has started hurting from carpel tunnel symptoms. This makes it harder to write with my pen. God, you have changed me even more than I could have imagined in such a short time, in this couple of months.

The freedom and grace that have been shown to me are overwhelming. My wife tells me every day that I am a new person. Without the journal entries to show it, I couldn't tell you what I have done for the past 12 years. It is like God helped me break through a door and out of the prison gate into an open field where I can see the light again. I was blind and trapped, but now I see!

I have been to hell and back again now, and I wonder why I was sometimes spared, but I know you, Lord, have been the driving force behind it all, with no real thanks to my efforts. The work of Satan's prison was being used to try and make me falter, but you prevailed in my life, God.

Where should I start the next phase of my life? I just finished a course on getting my life back from this world's clutches, and it feels good to be free from those medications. It feels even better seeing that God freed me and told me the truth, unlike what the world tried to tell me. They were telling me never to stop taking the medications because I was broken.

The world had me over a barrel with these medications. I was told at one point that God wanted me to be on the medications. I was told that God put doctors on the earth to help us get over depression and anxiety with medications. I was told that medications are the only thing that helps with ADD. That was the lie I was fed. The lie was that God couldn't break me out. I was stuck in that lie for twelve years because I listened to what the world said was wrong with me.

It's still hard for me to believe that I had to go through all of that and almost destroy my life because I trusted the wrong people who claimed to have my best interests in mind. It hurts me deeply. However, they were right about one thing: writing it down in a journal and sharing it with others saved my life. It allowed me to see how far I've come and reminded me of where it all began.

Ever since I started the road back program to recovery and got my life back from sin, I have struggled with the realization that others might not be able to break free as God has done for me. I have learned how to leave my problems at the cross of Jesus Christ. God has shown me how to nail sin so it won't return. Today starts a new chapter in my life that I look forward to.

I look forward to living my life with God and for Jesus Christ.

I still struggle with the imagery in my mind of my past behaviors popping into my head when I least expect it. Images of the people I had hurt while I was on the medications. Prostitutes, family members, friends, and some total strangers I took advantage of over time. I was not following God's will for my life at that time, and it all still haunts me when I least expect it. I have to admit Satan has a lot of tools in his belt to use on all of us.

Satan throws a lot of hammers at us when times are tough. He sends his worldly guard dogs after us when we leave the gate, hoping to wear the prisoner down to return to the jail cell of sin. He hates it when one of his prisoners goes free.

The best part about being freed from prison is that I no longer have to return there. I now have control of my thoughts, and the voices no longer entice me to hurt others again. Now that I am free, I can write about how God freed me to use my story to break others out of their prison cells of sin.

As I said before, one of the things that helped me to break free was journaling. I journaled every day I could with pencil and paper rather than typing it all out because my thoughts flowed much better than having interruptions from technology. I still have

ADD, and technology gets in the way of thinking when typing. If you want to cure your child or yourself of ADD, as it gets diagnosed that everyone has it, start writing things down and get away from technology as much as possible. Get your mind out on a page and let it flow to free up space for what is truly important.

I found that when I write down the truth on a page, Satan can't attack my mind. The truth is written where you can see it actively present, so I can't manipulate it to go a different way. Writing it out on a page makes it harder for Satan to tempt you with interruptions from your computer or notifications to interrupt your thoughts. I have learned not to allow Satan and the demons to get a foothold on my thoughts this way. If I see a weak spot in my life, I now take action to eliminate it by writing it down and comparing it with scripture and truth.

Sin is a cancer that needs to be aggressively addressed. Anything in our lives can be used for good or evil purposes. I am living proof of that. I want to choose the good and right things to do, but Satan wants to lie, steal, and destroy our lives. That is why it is important to know the truth so that it can set you free.

Today, I fully give my life to Christ so He can lead me where He wants me to go. I write this because that is what I have learned to do. I know this is what God is calling me to do, and I am choosing to love God, follow Jesus, and throw out my old way of living in sin. It will be hard, but God will work hard for me. I know I can always lay my sins at his feet and rest at the foot of the cross. I will wait for his instructions on what to do next. Amen!

4:01 AM

Yesterday, I sold my violent video games and decided to turn my life even deeper towards Jesus. I decided to do so because believing in and following Jesus Christ is a choice. That is the free will that God offers everyone. Everything else is predestined; either sin lures away our hearts and the world shows us shiny things, or Jesus and God, along with the Holy Spirit, lead your life to righteousness.

God, in three parts, if we choose to allow them, will dwell in us at any given time once we accept them. I am choosing to know nothing else, but Christ and Him crucified. What I mean by all this is simply this: Without Jesus in my life today, my past and future are nothing apart from knowing Him. He saved my life and marriage, and my heart now belongs to Him first and foremost. To give it to anything else is to let Satan win. Satan has lost any influence over my life because God's Holy Spirit is now taking up residence in my heart. Jesus will be in my life forever more.

I have decided to write my next book about the struggles of mental health and the false findings of medical professionals who I use to put my life and my trust into. I am going to tell the story of how Jesus took me away from being trapped by the drugs the doctors said would help me with depression, anxiety, and ADD and speak the truth about what is happening.

Jesus gave me my life back, so I am giving my life back to Jesus! I have seen the fight for human life on several fronts. Human trafficking is one of those fronts, but also mental health issues are another front that I am addressing. I have helped many people now, all of whom suffered for far too long in bondage or slavery to sin, and has shown me it is in my writing that God wants to use me the most. So, I will share this with the world. So be it. Amen!

9:50 AM

Today, I was aware of the attacks on my mind. I could feel the pull of Satan's grasp on me. Satan wants me to hire an escort. I even called a girl and made the appointment.

I then received a text from our red-headed friend, which made me realize I was under attack. I quickly responded that I was under attack from Satan.

I remember a bill collector calling me. They were harassing me for money before this. I felt money was out of my control after the call, so I wanted to act out. I knew I was under attack and needed to defuse the situation. I called my wife, discussed my dilemma, and immediately discussed our finances. I might have gone through with the appointment had I been on the medications still, but thanks be to God for pulling me out.

I wanted to blow up at my wife because she forgot to pay a bill she had created by purchasing clothes, but I didn't. It may be time to take back some of the financial responsibility from her and help her out. I know I am no longer going to act out with escorts anymore, but those temptations are going to continue to arise during hard times. I need to guard my heart from such attacks with truth and with other people I can trust.

My wife asked me to attend a meeting tonight, and I agreed that I should. I needed more insight into what God had in store for me, and my brothers in Christ are not helping because they are not where I am in healing right now. I might have to step it up with God's help. While at the insurance company, I am under constant attack, so I may have to do something about it.

I write in my journal daily because it makes me feel better. I have encouraged many people to do the same thing, but their excuses are always the same: "I need to improve my writing skills first." I find it interesting how God can bring people out of their shells and comfort zones to do what they were meant to do.

Today, I am praying for my mentor's family and friends from my recovery group. I pray that God will continue to use me to plant seeds and help grow their faith in Jesus. The family has already been curious about who Jesus is, and I believe God wants me to bring people to His glory. This is a goal I have for my life, but I must remember to leave everything in God's hands, as He has a far greater plan than I know. I hope to live long enough to see it play out.

I had a gout attack today, so I brought cherries to work with me. God willing, it will help some of the pain. My wife started back to work yesterday. She was on summer break. I can only hope that there were clerical errors in her pay raise. The value of her paycheck didn't change, so I was concerned that they didn't follow through with their end of the deal. I know we will be alright, but it makes life harder to pay the bills if we don't get her raised income.

Today has been amazing. I listened to scriptures and daily meditations that told me to be still and know He is God. It all held as the family I had been introduced to through my mentor and the church that hosted the Cross-Centered Mind course replied without my need to do anything. God works far better than I ever could do on my own. I am scared of offending the family and their culture to some degree. That is mostly because I still need to learn more about their culture. But I know that God will provide me with the answers.

God has put it on my heart to possibly ask my pastor to accompany us to the restaurant I picked so that I can get to know this family better. I will also ask my wife for advice because she is my spiritual partner, and I trust her opinion. All in all, God has blessed me in so many ways today.

My bible study lesson was a long lesson with much reading that needed to happen. I am grateful I stepped back and let it take me two days to read. Yesterday, my heart was just not in it. I was feeling lost for some reason. I prayed that God would continue to use me and bring me deeper into his ministry over my life so I can live life to its fullest. I also need to transfer the car insurance for our van tonight so we can rest easier on the loan. I hope God will provide me with the solution and what I need to improve my life. I am a huge target right now for Satan, and I need to go to the armor of God for protection. Amen!

I missed writing in my journal this weekend because I was so busy. I watched my two nieces for my sister-in-law and her husband. We also went to a great church service at work and took a family out to eat at a Mongolian grill.

The family is from India and moved to the United States after being persecuted six years ago by a dictator king of Nepal. I discovered that one of the daughters works with me at the insurance company, and I have often helped her with technical support issues over the phone. I also spoke with my recovery friend about getting the family a Hindi or Nepali-translated bible for easier reading. I hope that God might help me trust Him more in my own life so that I can do more for families such as these kind people. I will also check with my pastor about a church family that speaks Hindi and might take them in and teach them God's ways. I pray that God will keep me focused on Him and help me lead others further as I am being led myself.

Chapter 13

2015

The Start of Prayer and Fasting

"Stop depriving one another, except by agreement for a time, so that you may devote yourselves to prayer, and come together again so that Satan will not tempt you because of your lack of self-control." 1 Corinthians 7:5 NASB

After breaking free from such horrors, God showed me a different path. One where I wasn't going into ministry but would show the world Him and the grace He showed me before all men. My journals are based on a study I went through about prayer and getting right with God and His word. And if all of this sounds like a different person, I have been made new in Jesus Christ.

Sometimes, I wonder why God puts me in such situations. I had my wife turn up her ringer volume only to have it pushed over to mute. I attempted to call her and received no answer, so I thought that maybe she was hurt or had another seizure. I found out halfway home from the beginning of the workday that it was muted.

Then I got a call from my dopey friend's girlfriend saying that they were through, that she was going home to be with her parents, and that she was taking their child with her. She said that my dopey friend would never see his son again. What a day, Lord!

Have you ever had a day like this? I have been up a creek without a paddle, and God's help seems never to come. I have to say that without God's word and God's help, I wouldn't have anything to stand on right now.

Today, he told me everything would be alright and that He would give me the words to help my friend's situation. God's help comes through quickly and always on time.

On my way home, I received a call that all was better and that I didn't need to come over to talk with my dopey friend and his girlfriend about their situation. God truly does work miracles. Then my wife called me back and apologized for muting her phone. Amen!

If I was ever to learn anything from my journals and stop listening to the world, I needed to shut the windows of my apartment. I needed to tune the world out and let God's love guide me. I am on my bed, typing out my journals, listening to children scream and curse at each other. They are no older than nine years old. I am closing the window now to heal my soul and turn my life over to God's care.

God fully understands your situation and is ready to impart timely wisdom. Prayer is Satan's demise. If God's word is like water for our lives, then prayer is like oxygen. There is a never-ending need: prayer comes first. It is not an emergency parachute but must be primary to living out God's purpose.

I pray for my dopey friend and his girl-friend to find peace in you, Lord. I pray God will teach them who He is and that their hearts will turn to Him. I pray that you will provide them with everything they need. I pray that they will raise their son in your ways. I pray that they stop fighting each other and fight for their lives to be together.

Praying for wisdom is a daily habit and a source for developing our prayer strategies. When we pray for wisdom, we invite God into our day to give us supernatural power over our thoughts and problems. Praying in the offensive means praying for the light, love, and truth. Don't just pray against hardships, but pray for blessings. We need to pray offensively, as in Philippians 1:9-11.

Peter never prayed preemptively, so he wept bitterly instead. We must pray before entering the battlefield for the battle's outcome, God's protection, and the whole armor to be put on us.

We need to know Satan's game plans and how he is going to attack us. He uses the same methods, and we can use prayer to defend against all of them.

Praying for our families should start with specifics and power in Jesus' name. Jesus is the head of the church, just as husbands are the head of the household. Jesus is the truly ultimate head. Both spouses should pray for a sense of protective passion for marriage's primary function: marriage being a flesh-and-blood representation of the gospel of your children, your friends, and everyone who knows you.

As I grew in my prayer life, God slowly peeled away the scars and created a new person in my heart. I no longer lived for myself but chose to help others fight to strengthen their relationship with God and each other. I rebuilt my trust with my wife over time. We could no longer have children due to the abuse, the high amounts of sexual activity I had pushed on my body, and the abuse I endured growing up. I had started having gout attacks daily, and I had pain when going to the restroom. It turned out that I had a blockage, causing my body to become toxic and not release the uric acids from my body. God had other plans for us as believers. Here are the rest of my journal entries for 2015.

God, Grant me repentance from all my sins, especially those that deal with the shame and guilt of the lustful thoughts and gluttony. Please help me remove all of my pride in my heart for anything in this world. Let all of my pride be found in you.

Help me to love my family as you have first loved me. Bring me to a greater understanding of who I am in you. Keep me alert daily to temptations to sinful things, and be there for me as I know you are when I can't see the sins before me. Please carry me away from those temptations and guide me to your will for my life.

You, Lord, have overcome everything through your Son, Jesus Christ. Please provide me a way out whenever I am tempted and help me to see that way. Lord, please help bring people who want to know you more into my life that you want me to guide them to your will over their lives. Prepare your way in me that it helps to bring others to your love, mercy, glory, and peace. Show me how this works in your plan for my life, Lord God almighty. In Jesus' name, I pray. Amen!

Today, I read from John 6. One thing that stuck out to me was that Jesus had disciples who left his side and returned to their old ways. It was because they didn't believe that the flesh and blood of Jesus Christ could bring them eternal life. They needed to eat the flesh and drink the blood, and they thought it was too much and that Jesus was crazy. They stopped short of the goal and chose not to follow Jesus further.

However, the twelve were still with him because they left everything behind to follow Jesus. They had nothing to return to and gave all they had to trust God, who chose them to follow him because He searched their hearts and knew them, including Judas.

Judas betrayed Jesus and God, but God knew it would happen. That reminded me that God knew Satan's motives at the beginning and how pride would allow Satan to fall. Satan wanted to be like God and betrayed God and tried to take God's place. All this talk about food and my fasting day made me want to eat.

God, please satisfy my hunger and fill me with your word today. I will not want anything else in my life, so that I won't turn away from your presence. Lord, lead me away from temptation and keep my mind and heart close to your life-giving love, word, spirit, and the Son Jesus Christ. I pray in His name. Amen!

Today, the world discussed how yesterday was "Back to the Future Day." I wonder how people aren't more in awe of who God is and where we are being led by this world's lack of God's care. Not that God lacks anything, but that we have all gone astray from how we see God in our lives. We don't look to God the same way the disciples did in the Bible some 2,000 years ago when the bible was written.

Thank you, God, for being so patient and loving to all of your creation. Help us all see you before it's too late. Remind us all of who you are daily. Your love for us all humbles us to look to you again. Think Big! Think creation. Think Universe!

Then, compare our lives to who the creator is and how much God loves us in the grand scheme of things. It is not that we are unique because we have been given life, but that we are given life and that God chose to love us, His creation, and send His son down to provide us with just a glimpse of His power over all of the universe. How insignificant we all look to the rest of the Universe on a scale that we can't even begin to fathom.

If there is life on other planets, we can't see it. Humans have a huge ego, and we truly disprove God's word and outsee God. We try to imagine creation without God, and it is unimaginable. The idea that God doesn't exist for me is unimaginable, given what we can see in front of our faces. When we look at the stars alone, it is impossible not to see God in them. Amen! Jesus! Amen!

I am noting this from reading John 9. Interestingly, Jesus always seemed to heal people on the Sabbath day. This got Him in trouble with the Pharisees, the religious leaders who condemned Him to death. The people Jesus healed testified to His healing ability, but people still didn't believe in His works or words.

His word was also from God. Were the Pharisees condemning God for not resting on the day of rest? Maybe they were. Another thing I just thought of is that while Jesus was performing miracles from God on the Sabbath, the Pharisees were working on the Sabbath to condemn Jesus.

It was their job to uphold the law of Moses, so by performing their jobs on the Sabbath day, they did the same thing Jesus did. This was all in the sight of God, the Son, and today, the Holy Spirit convicts our hearts when we sin. One thing I do know is that I was blind, but now I see, and it was Jesus who set me free. Amen!

After reading John 20, I found this noteworthy: When Jesus returned from the dead, He showed himself to all the disciples except Thomas. I don't believe this was a mistake. God reveals Himself to us in His time and at the right time.

We must remain at His feet and let Him be the Head of our lives. When we do, we show faith in His word and trust in His presence. His word then brings out truth, and when His truth and spirit flow over us, they bring forward His Holy Spirit. Life is born again in us even before the Pentecost of change. Boldness springs up, and then we realize that, indeed, He is alive! I believe this with my whole heart. I pray for this in everyone's life. In Jesus' name, I pray this. Amen!

Chapter 14

Conclusion

The rest of the story!

"FOR I DETERMINED TO KNOW NOTHING AMONG YOU EXCEPT JESUS CHRIST AND HIM CRUCIFIED."
1 CORINTHIANS 2:2 NASB

God calls all of us as human beings to follow Him and His will for our lives. One of the greatest things that helped me to overcome my addiction to pornography, objectifying women, and drugs was to cut things out of my life completely. The further away I grew from those things that held me captive, what brought me out of their lure of power over my life was fleeing from them. You need to take extreme measures against sin. Sin is deadly to the soul and sometimes deadly to our physical bodies. It wasn't an easy escape, but it was worth every scar to flee it.

From 2014 on, I stopped listening to much of what the world taught me because the information was wrong. I started hearing God's Word more. I stopped listening to secular music; I stopped watching many television shows I used to watch religiously. These things were feeding my mind with evil intent. Shows like CSI, Criminal Minds, South Park, and various shows that say sin is not that bad triggered something in my mind and kept me trapped in fear and doubt along with the medications, keeping my focus on things I didn't want to focus on.

I decided to follow God fully and not halfheartedly. This meant I didn't stop reading my Bible without hearing God speak to my heart. Dedicating my life to Christ also meant being involved in my church family's life every day of the week, and not just on Sunday. It meant giving up myself to help others and seeing what God had assigned me through to completion. I had to learn to keep my word on everything that I did. It meant no more lying to myself or others and telling the truth about everything in my life. I couldn't break any more promises and would always be where I said I would be.

Accountability and transparency are two keys to fully trusting God in our lives. God says that if we are lukewarm, He will spit us out of His mouth. "Revelations 3:16". I chose not to be lukewarm anymore. I felt God called me to write my testimony and share my life with others, so I have been working hard to ensure it was with Him in mind the entire time. He is the One Who deserves all of the credit. He did all of the hard stuff for me. I laid down at His feet and allowed Him to make the changes. I let Him be the Creator as I remained the created. This allowed me to draw so very close to Him every day.

As I drew closer to God, I could tell He was drawing closer to me. As I read His Word more and more daily, the words in the scriptures healed my soul. The idea that some people believe God doesn't exist anymore still baffles me. However, I have proof that He was always there for me. My journals, experiences, and life now all prove who God says He is.

The moments in my life where I was abused, neglected, addicted, or even hurting others have no more power in my life, thanks to God's love. How did this happen? Is it real, you might ask? Am I going to go back to the old ways and be like the hypocrites that you might see in churches or the Bible? Will I be tempted to go back to my old ways? I asked those questions for many years after I got off the medications. Am I still in control, or is God in the driver's seat? "God is in control of my destiny, and He is a much better driver and forecaster of where I need to go than anyone in the world has ever directed me."

I hold the scripture from Psalm 23 very close to my heart today because God does lead me beside the still waters. The valley of the shadow of death still gets dark at times, but they are only shadows of death and not truthfully death. This might be scary to some, but I know who is casting the shadow. God holds me so close today that I do not need to return to those old ways.

He has given me more freedom and clarity than I have ever experienced. Allowing God's Word to guide me and living in His presence is far more peaceful and fulfilling than anything else I have tried to use to fill that void.

God has placed people in my path who hold me accountable for my actions. I also hold myself accountable for my actions through accountability software, blocking sites not in my best interest, and seeking forgiveness when I make mistakes. I have also become more self-aware of the medications I am prescribed, as I have had some setbacks using various medications. Since accepting Him, I have worked hard to cling to Him and His Word daily and no longer take medications to cope with anxiety or depression. The more I trust Him with my life, the more I see how deep His love is.

I don't know how to explain it other than to say that God is who He says He is and is all-powerful. Even when I was in the mental health facility, God was there. When I was being abused, God knew He could use it to help others get past it by telling my story. God knew He would later free me and show me who He is. He never lets us go, even in the worst of times in our lives.

I encourage anyone reading this to push out any doubt from your mind. Tell Satan to flee from you in Jesus' Name. Start reading your Bible. Get close to God and learn from Him directly. Get into God's Word daily, at least three times a day. God's Word has the power to change your life. Listen to Him speak to your heart. Don't do what most people do. Don't be normal. Don't just read scripture from the beginning to the end. Let it penetrate your heart.

Find the subject matters you are dealing with and read those chapters first. God wants to take those obstacles out of your life. Take it a day at a time and listen to God's Word penetrate your mind. Turn off those outside world influences and only listen to God's Word. There is worldly wisdom and Godly wisdom. Choose Godly wisdom every time. He created us. He knows what we were made to do.

This means eliminating all musical influences, including Christian music, for a time. Step away from news media, social media, video games, and even your cell phone for about a month. Use this time to read God's Word and let it sink into your heart and mind.

Start with the Psalms. I read a chapter of Proverbs every day for 31 days and then looked up subjects I struggled with in the Bible index. Read your Bible daily, at least three times a day, and see how much closer you will come to knowing Who God is and how much closer you will be to the Creator of the universe at the end of those 30 days. Truly, it is a good thing for your life.

In separating from the mental health medications and drugs I was on over the years, I have not gone back. I still see a Christian counselor for guidance about life issues, but we all need counseling. Even pastors and priests need guidance from Godly people. We shouldn't go through these battles alone. What I went through to get away from the medications and mental health rhetoric was a lot of pain and struggles. I even lost my job over it. And yet God got me through it through trusting in Him, reading scripture, and having someone there as a mentor to help guide me because I was flying blind. Now that I am through it, however, I can share an experience with the world, one that God led me all the way. Now that I am through it all, I can truly see. That is the change that Jesus made in me.

As for the escort services and prostitutes and sleeping around on my wife, we are still married and working through the tough stuff, but God even had His hand in this. He has healed our relationship. He brought both of us people who are great friends today and still hold us accountable. They know my back story and don't judge me over my past. They know that I am with Christ and that He is with me. Those friends continue to encourage us to keep our faith and help keep our marriage strong.

While I do believe that sin is sin, and whatever we might call sin, whether it be addiction or any other label, we all fall short of God's glory, and only He can redeem us from those things that hold us down. We need to be vigilant to stay the course. Some people who know my story might say it was unprecedented what I did to my wife, but I assure you that forgiveness heals a great multitude of sins. Many of us who are hurting or have hurt others need grace. Without it, there is no hope for healing.

Being off the medications has truly healed me from a lot of my sinful behaviors. The medications have changed my mind to some degree. Doctors still do not know how all the medicines we put in our bodies change our behaviors. I would encourage you, if you are seeking help in doing what I have done and trying to get off of psychiatric medicines, to seek professional help. Pray hard for several days about your specific situation and look for assistance in getting the help. Please don't do it alone.

A very good friend of mine saw my success in this matter and decided to skip the program, do "The Road Back" program, and skip God's part. That may have been what cost him his life. As I said before, this was an act of God, not mine. It is nothing short of a miracle that I am still alive today. If you would like to seek help in this area, please go to www.settingcaptivesfree.com and speak with the ministry team there to see how you can break free from your mental health issues.

It is important to approach the issue that you are currently facing with a constructive mindset. As you pray about your situation, it is important to consider that some people may need to remain on their medications and that each case is unique. While my experience has been described as a miracle by some therapists and doctors, they have also noted that I should have remained on medication for a little longer and that my quick withdrawal should have resulted in side effects. It is important to note that some doctors may push you to go back on medication, so it is crucial to know your doctor well and seek multiple opinions before making any decisions. Keep an open mind and a positive attitude as you navigate this difficult situation.

Many lives have been lost or affected by mental health-related issues in the United States alone. Many more are affected every day around the world. God sees us all as His children and wants us to return to Him, but it is in His time, not ours. We should run and not look back to get to Him if the opportunity presents itself. Wait for God to make the first move, but be alert and wait.

As for the area of childhood sexual abuse in my life, I have made amends with my brother and his family. Some things still need to work themselves out with God's help, but ultimately, God controls everything. Simply put, how it works out is amazing. I am now helping men and women overcome sexually abusive past behaviors. I assist homeless men and women in seeking help to heal from the abuse of their pasts.

The scars of abuse are very deep and cut to the heart, but God heals those scars over time. Eventually, God will remove those memories completely, and only a picture of their existence will remain. Those events don't have to define us as people of God. They become pictures in our minds and our testimonies to share with others struggling with what we went through.

Every time a piece of my past plays out in my head, I can now picture it being nailed to the cross and Jesus taking it away. He keeps His promise to take it away from my mind and heart. The Bible says Jesus takes it away from us as far as the East is from the West. Jesus tears it apart and takes it away from me, and I will never have to look back on it again.

At one point, I was told there seemed to be no hope in my first book about my childhood and that God could never produce anything good out of this story. I am living proof that God can use anyone or anything, even a childhood sexual abuse survivor turned sex addict and molester into a follower of Christ who turned his life around to help others heal from their pasts. It is only by the grace of God that I am alive today to tell this story and hopefully help others seek God differently.

We need to face our fears head-on. Never give up hope when God is involved in your life. God always shows up. No matter who tells you that you are worthless, that you don't matter, that you are a sick and twisted and demented person, when you invite Jesus into your heart and accept Him as your Lord and Savior and believe without a doubt that He is Who He says He is, then you can say that, "The old person you knew no longer exists because Christ lives in me, and I am a new creation." Know that Jesus Christ died for everyone on the earth to redeem us all from the pit of hell. No sin, too great or small, can keep Jesus from us if we seek Him out wholeheartedly. He covered all of our sins.

In 2016, the U.S. government signed into law a bill that would eliminate the use of websites to promote the use of escort services, prostitution, and human trafficking. This has amounted to the arrest of several thousands of criminals, and this has saved the lives of countless victims of human trafficking and sexual abuse victims. While sex trafficking is still a global issue, people around the world are making the issue more prevalent, and people are starting to take notice.

Having these sites taken down has been a prayer answered, keeping me safe from harming myself or others. While medications were my main issue, I acknowledge my role in my harmful behavior and am working daily to make amends. With God by your side, nothing is impossible. All obstacles will eventually disappear, sometimes quickly and sometimes slowly, but they will go away through His power. So you might as well face it!

Milton Keynes UK
Ingram Content Group UK Ltd.
UKHW021818251124
451531UK00007B/52